CC
GE

Population Geography

Hazel R. Barrett BA (Hons) MA PhD

Lecturer in Geography
Derbyshire College of Higher Education

Oliver & Boyd

Acknowledgements

The authors and publishers wish to thank all those who gave their permission to reproduce copyright material in this book.
Information regarding sources is given in the captions.

Cover illustrated by Lynda McNee
Maps and diagrams drawn by Tim Smith

Dedicated to Mum, Dad and Pieter

Oliver & Boyd
Edinburgh Gate,
Harlow,
Essex CM20 2JE
An Imprint of Longman Group Ltd

ISBN 0 05 004507 5
First published 1992
Seventh impression 1998

Printed in Singapore through Addison Wesley Longman China Limited

The Publisher's policy is to use paper manufactured from
sustainable forests.

Contents

Editor's Note

An encouraging feature in geographical education in recent years has been the convergence taking place of curriculum thinking and thinking at the academic frontiers of the subject. In both, stress has been laid on the necessity for conceptual approaches and the use of information as a means to an end rather than as an end in itself.

The central purpose of this series is to bear witness to this convergence. In each text the *key ideas* are identified, chapter by chapter. These ideas are in the form of propositions which, with their component concepts and the inter-relations between them, make up the conceptual frameworks of the subject. The key ideas provide criteria for selecting content for the teacher, and in cognitive terms help the student to retain what is important in each unit. Most of the key ideas are linked with assignments, designed to elicit evidence of achievements of basic understanding and ability to apply this understanding in new circumstances through engaging in problem-solving exercises.

While the series is not specifically geared to any particular 'A' level examination syllabus, indeed it is intended for use in geography courses in universities, polytechnics and in colleges of higher education as well as in the sixth form, it is intended to go some way towards meeting the needs of those students preparing for the more radical advanced geography syllabuses.

It is hoped that the texts contain the academic rigour to stretch the most able of such candidates, but at the same time provide a clear enough exposition of the basic ideas to provide intellectual stimulus and social and/or cultural relevance for those who will not be going on to study geography in higher education. To this end, a larger selection of assignments and readings is provided than perhaps could be used profitably by all students. The teacher is the best person to choose those which most nearly meet his or her students' needs.

W.E. Marsden
University of Liverpool.

Preface

In the forty years since population geography became a clearly distinguishable sub-discipline of geography, it has matured and progressed from the identification and description of population patterns to an examination and discussion of the processes responsible for those patterns. This book explores the current issues and concepts in population geography with reference to detailed case studies which include new interpretations of historical population trends as well as analysis of recent demographical patterns. The book uses the most recent sources of quantitative data and draws on current debate within the subject to provide an up-to-date analysis of population geography.

There are many people who deserve thanks for their encouragement and help in the preparation and writing of this book, in particular the library and geography staff at Derbyshire College of Higher Education. A special thankyou must be given to my parents for their invaluable support.

Hazel R. Barrett

1 *Population Distribution and Carrying Capacity*

Introduction

Population geography is the study of spatial variations in the distribution, composition, migration and growth of populations. It is this concern with spatial patterns that distinguishes population geography from the closely related but statistically based discipline of demography. In the last twenty years the boundaries between geography and other disciplines interested in population matters, such as economics, sociology, history, psychology and biology, as well as demography, have become less distinguishable. As a result, population geography can no longer be regarded as being exclusively concerned with spatial distributions. Population geographers are increasingly attempting to explain the patterns and distributions they have identified. In doing this the sub-discipline has moved away from description and statistical analysis. Today much more emphasis is given to the processes which create and modify population patterns. In attempting to explain spatial variations in population characteristics, population geography embraces almost every other aspect of geography, including economic and historical geography, as well as climatology and biogeography. As such, population geography is regarded by many as the core of the wider discipline of geography, linking the traditionally separate elements of physical and human geography.

A. Population Distribution

In 1985 the United Nations estimated that the world's population stood at over 4.8 billion. This is equivalent to an average population density of 36 people per square kilometre, or each human being having on average 2.8 hectares of living space. In reality, however, these figures are meaningless as people are very unevenly distributed in space and the distribution is undergoing continuous change.

Figure 1.1 demonstrates the spatial distribution of the world's population, showing clearly the uneven nature of population densities. The map highlights four major concentrations of population. These are located in Eastern and Southern Asia, Europe and North-Eastern USA. In addition, pockets of high density are evident in

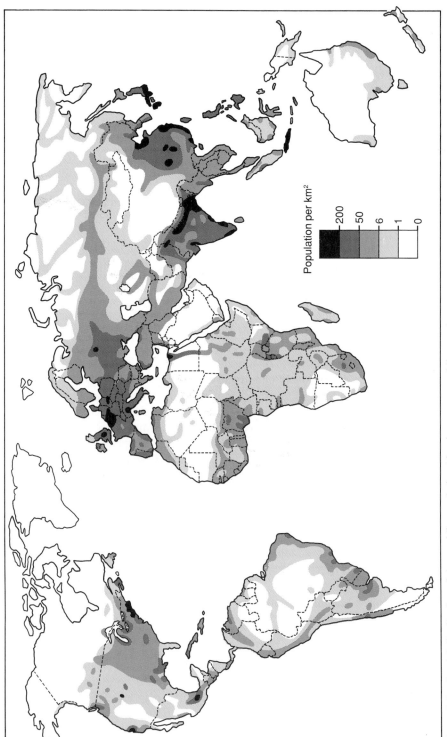

Figure 1.1 Spatial distribution of the world's population (density per square kilometre)

Population per km²

200
50
6
1
0

Table 1.1   Total population and population density by major world region, 1985
(Source: UN Demographic Yearbook, 1985)

	Population Millions	%	Population Density per km²
Africa	555	11.5	18
N. America	264	5.4	12
S. America	405	8.4	20
E. Asia	1250	25.8	106
S. Asia	1456	30.1	129
W. Asia	113	2.3	25
Europe	492	10.2	100
Oceania	25	0.5	3
USSR	279	5.8	12
Total	4839	100.0	36

the Nile Valley, California, coastal regions of South America, central Mexico, parts of West and Southern Africa and the metropolitan areas of Australia. From the map it appears that people prefer to live on the edges of the continents rather than in the interior. Population densities are also low in desert, polar and mountainous regions.

Calculations done by the eminent population geographer John Clarke confirm these visual impressions. He estimates that 75% of the world's population lives within 1000 kilometres of the sea, with almost two-thirds living within 500 kilometres of the coast. He also calculates that 80% of the world's population lives in areas that are under 500 metres above sea level, with 56% living in areas below 200 metres above sea level. Clarke also states that the majority of the world's population lives in the much larger land mass of the northern hemisphere with over 80% of the world's people living between latitude 20° N and 60° N. Less than 10% of the world's population lives in the southern hemisphere.

The uneven nature of global population distribution is confirmed by Table 1.1. This table demonstrates that over 58% of the world's population lives in Asia, with 11.5% in Africa and over 10% in Europe. However, within these regions there are large regional disparities, with population densities in Asia, for example, ranging from 25 to 129 per square kilometre. The lowest population densities are to be found in Oceania, USSR and North America. Population geographers are interested in explaining population distributions. This involves examining the processes and factors that are responsible for the patterns shown on Figure 1.1.

B. The Process of Population Change

Population change is the result of the interaction of three processes: births, deaths and migration. These are known as the *dynamic components* of population change

= POPULATION

Figure 1.2   Components of population change

and are the principle focus of population geography. These dynamic components can interact in such a way that population numbers may increase, decrease or remain stable (see Figure 1.2). Populations will increase in number when births exceed deaths and in-migrations exceed out-migrations. Similarly, population numbers will fall when deaths exceed births and out-migrations exceed in-migrations. The interaction of these components is affected by spatial factors, particularly the ability to make a living, as well as socio-economic and technological changes through time. It is the spatial and temporal interaction of these dynamic components which produces changes in population numbers, density and composition, and is responsible for the present-day pattern of population distribution discussed in section A. Each of these dynamic components is discussed in detail in Chapters 3, 4 and 5.

C. Factors affecting Population Distribution

The overriding factor affecting population distribution is the ability of a population to make a satisfactory living. This in turn may be dependent on ecological factors, as well as socio-economic and political considerations. The main factors affecting population distributions are shown in Figure 1.3. The relative importance of each factor will vary both in space and time.

Figure 1.3   Main factors and processes affecting population size and distribution

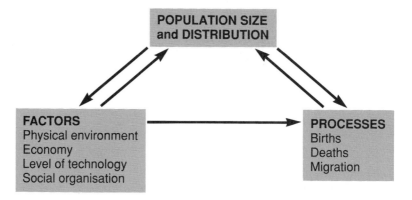

1. Ecological (physical) factors

All human beings require certain resources in order to live. These include, oxygen, water and food, warmth and living space. The human requirements for each of these ecological factors is shown in Table 1.2. However, it should be remembered that the human population is biologically very adaptable, as evidenced by Inuits, Desert Bedouins and Andean Indians, who all manage to make a living in cold, arid and mountainous locations respectively.

Table 1.2 Ecological necessities for human life

Oxygen	After adjustment human beings can live in altitudes as high as 5000 metres, without supplementary supplies.
Water	Fundamental to life. About ten tonnes of drinking water per tonne of living tissue is required each year by human beings.
Warmth	Without clothing and shelter humans can only withstand temperatures of less than –5 °C and temperatures in excess of 40 °C for short periods of time. The optimum temperature range for humans is 10–30 °C.
Food	Human beings need certain nutrients and calorific intake to maintain a healthy life, although people can survive many weeks without food.
Living space	Humans find it difficult to live on glaciers, shifting sands and rough rocky surfaces. Otherwise they can live almost anywhere, as long as the above factors are provided.

Plate 1.1   A fur-clad Inuit hunter in Northern Canada demonstrates that human beings are highly adaptable to extreme physical conditions. (Photograph: B & C Alexander)

Plate 1.2   When physical conditions such as water, light, nutrients and temperature are controlled as in a greenhouse, food can be grown almost anywhere on the earth's surface. Here in Andalusia, Spain, greenhouses enable fruit and vegetables to be grown all year round. Much of this produce is exported to other parts of Europe, allowing us to enjoy exotic fruits, such as strawberries, at all times of the year. (Photograph: J. Allan Cash Ltd)

Although there are clear physical constraints on where people can live, human beings can live almost anywhere on the earth's surface, using technology and imported resources. Human beings can even live for long periods of time in space, provided the basic biological requirements are supplied to them.

Ecological factors can have both a limiting and an enhancing effect on the distribution of human populations. Favourable physical factors such as good soil and flat terrain can attract people to an area and help support high densities, whereas unfavourable conditions, such as cold climates and high altitudes, repel people. However, it must be stressed that physical factors are inextricably linked to economic factors. Many physical constraints can be overcome, if economically attractive, by the importation and supplementation of resources from other areas. For example, deserts can be made to bloom and to support people by the use of irrigation technology, but this demands a high level of social organisation and technological skill.

It is difficult to state a clear-cut relationship between population density and physical factors because of the interplay of socio-economic considerations. The major factor determining population distribution is the ability of people to make a living within the ecological constraints discussed previously. Human numbers tend to correspond to areas with an adequate climate and fertile soil, as well as areas with favourable energy and mineral endowments.

(a) Climate and soils

The effects of climate on habitability are both direct and indirect. The major clusters of population are in the sub-tropical and mid-latitudes, and the sub-arctic,

12

polar, arid and semi-arid climatic zones are thinly populated. Because climate is a fundamental force shaping vegetation and soil patterns, the three tend to coincide, making it difficult to isolate climatic variables as concerns population distribution.

Areas of cold climates tend to repel human populations, thus the high northern latitudes, which comprise 10% of the earth's land area, are home to only a few thousand people. However, this may not simply be the result of low temperatures, but may also represent the low productive capacity of the area due to the short growing season. By contrast, high temperatures attract human beings. This is perhaps because warmer climates indirectly promote rapid vegetation growth, permit the practice of multiple cropping, allow the production of a large range of crops and reduce the requirements for clothing and shelter. Warm temperatures also stimulate the rapid propagation of insects, fungi and bacteria, which can all harm human, animal and plant health. Nevertheless, technological advances can overcome some of these problems, maintaining the attractiveness of the areas to human habitation.

The availability of water, usually from precipitation, is an important consideration for human habitation, not only to fulfil the biological needs of human beings but also to enable animals and plants to exist. Areas of little precipitation impose a low limit on population numbers, unless reserves of underground water can be utilised or water is imported from elsewhere. However, this requires a certain level of technology to be feasible on a large scale.

The attractiveness of a region for human occupation may depend partly on the quality of the soil. Some soils are not able to support large agricultural populations, for example, highly weathered lateritic soils which are found in many tropical areas. These nutrient-deficient soils are not suitable for intensive continuous cultivation of annual crops or even tree crops, therefore population densities are limited in such areas. By contrast, areas with deep alluvial deposits, for example the Ganges, Mekong and Yellow River Deltas, have high nutrient values and can support dense populations. Alluvial soils support a larger proportion of the world's population than any other of the main categories of soil. Clearly, agriculturally based societies dependent on the land for their living will favour more fertile regions.

(b) Energy and minerals

As the technological skills and level of social organisation of human populations has increased, sources of energy and minerals have gained in economic value and importance. As a result, people have settled in areas to exploit these resources. These resources have therefore exercised a powerful influence upon population distributions and densities. Coal in particular has had an important impact on population patterns, especially in Western Europe. In Britain the coalfield cities grew dramatically in the eighteenth and nineteenth centuries, as a result of the exploitation of coal as a source of energy to power industry. The close relationship between the iron and steel industry and coal as a form of energy enhanced the attractiveness of coal fields to industry and to people seeking employment. Cities such as Birmingham, which had been small villages before the industrial revolution, expanded into large manufacturing centres, whilst other urban areas such as

Scunthorpe and Corby were founded on the exploitation and processing of iron and steel. Coalfields therefore acted as a magnet to population in the eighteenth and nineteenth centuries, and as a result of historical inertia these areas still contain some of the highest population densities in the country. In this century, by contrast, the exploitation of oil and natural gas has been less significant in altering population patterns. This is primarily due to the fact that oil and gas are relatively easy to transport, and that many production sites are in unattractive locations.

Minerals, especially valuable deposits such as diamonds and gold, have in the past had a significant impact on population distributions. For example, the California gold rush of the mid-nineteenth century saw the movement of large numbers of people into the western states of USA. Likewise the discovery of gold in Australia had a similar impact on population patterns. However, in the twentieth century improved transportation technology has meant that mineral deposits exercise only a minor influence on population patterns. Nevertheless, the impact of certain high value deposits can affect population distributions, especially in areas of low population density, not only by attracting a permanent population but also by the establishment of migratory flows of workers.

Although energy and minerals have played an important role in determining past population patterns, the advance of technology and social organisation means that valuable resources can now be exploited without necessarily having a profound impact on population patterns. In fact, many sources of energy and minerals, such as nuclear power stations and large-scale mining operations, now repel people rather than attract them.

2. Socio-economic factors

It is generally agreed that the more complex a society becomes, the less directly physical factors influence the distribution of its population. Non-physical factors have a very important bearing on the distribution of people, and can result in physical constraints being overcome. Socio-economic considerations such as the level of technology attained by a society and the type of economic activity and social organisation adopted by groups of people can be equally if not more important than physical factors in determining population distributions. The impact of technology is of major significance, since it can affect the type of economic activity undertaken by a population, as well as influencing social organisation. These three factors are inextricably linked. As such, isolating the impact of any one factor upon population distributions is difficult.

(a) Level of technology

The ability of a population to make a satisfactory living will obviously depend on the level of social organisation and technology achieved by that group. This varies not only through time, but also spatially. It is these social considerations which help to explain the spatial differences in population density between areas of similar physical and resource characteristics. Recognising the importance of technology to

14

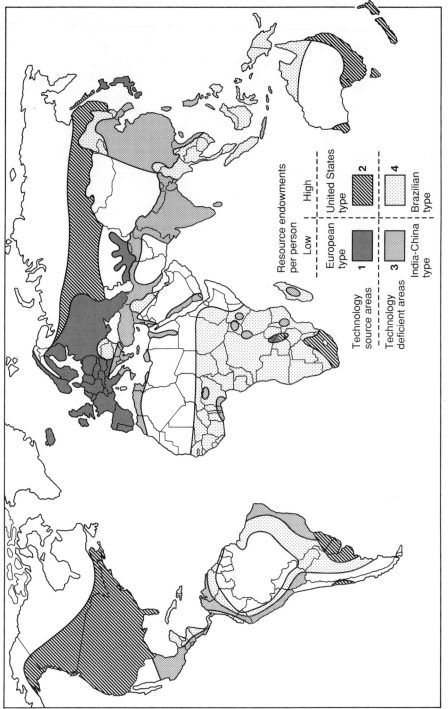

Figure 1.4 Ackerman's global classification of technology – resource regions (Source: Adams, Abler & Gould, 1971)

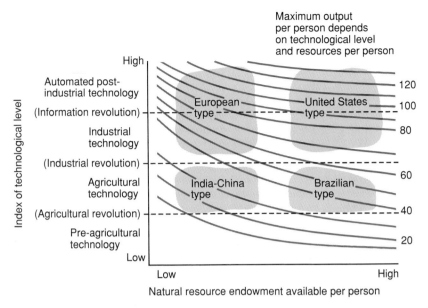

Figure 1.5 Technological levels and available resources per person, according to Ackerman's classification (Source: Adams, Abler & Gould, 1971)

population distribution, Edward Ackerman in 1967 published a classification of major global regions according to resource endowment and level of technology.

Ackerman identified five basic regional types: the European, United States, Brazilian, India-China and Arctic-Desert resource/technology regions. The first four of these types embrace the majority of the world's population and are shown in Figure 1.4. Each category has distinct resource and technology characteristics which distinguish it from the other types. These can be divided into those regions that enjoy a high level of technology and those that are technology deficient (see Figure 1.5).

The technology rich regions are the European and United States types. The European type region is one where although the natural resource endowment is low per person, the level of technology is high. This enables technology to be exported and high population densities to be supported at a good standard of living. The United States type region has both a high natural resource base and a high level of technology, once again providing a high standard of living for its population. By contrast the last three categories are technology-deficient and are often reliant on the previous two regions for innovations. The Brazilian type region, although having a high resource base has a low level of technology, and thus the ability to increase living standards and to support a larger population is limited. The most disadvantaged regions are those classified as of the India-China type (often referred to as the Egyptian type due to the technological advances made in India and China since 1967). These regions have a poor natural resource base and a very low level of technology. They tend to be the most economically disadvantaged areas, which in association with very high population densities often results in populations with a

16

very basic standard of living. The fifth category identified by Ackerman is the Arctic-Desert type. This, like the previous category, includes regions with few potential resources and a low level of technology. However, this category differs from the previous one in that the Arctic-Desert category supports a very low population density.

The Ackerman classification demonstrates that although a natural resource base is an important factor in determining population numbers and standards of living, other factors, including technology, determine the ability of a society to supply its population with a *satisfactory* standard of living. Technology is an important factor influencing population distribution and density. New techniques employed by a group of people may open up new areas for human habitation, for example, by the use of irrigation techniques, or may increase productivity, allowing a group to support larger numbers. At the same time technology can have a direct impact on the dynamic components of population change, altering population growth and composition. For example, contraceptive technology can give populations the ability to control the number of births and medical advances can increase life expectancy.

(b) Economic activity and social organisation

As the level of technology increases within a society so does the complexity of social organisation. This enables groups of people to diversify their economies, resulting in agriculture and fishing becoming relatively less important than trade and manufacturing. This shift in economic emphasis through time has had a significant effect on population distributions. The spatial distribution of an agricultural population will be totally different from that of a population engaged primarily in manufacturing, trade, fishing or mining.

The growth of world trade, together with the development of manufacturing and service industries, has altered the pattern of population distribution within most countries. The result has been an increased concentration of people in suitably located urban areas. Populations reliant on trade must be located on a strategically located commodity trading route, in order to be successful. For example, Singapore is in an excellent position to exploit the shipping trade between the Indian and Pacific Oceans. Its success has been aided by a large natural, deep, sheltered anchorage.

The distribution of population is highly dependent on the distribution of economic activities. As many jobs in the manufacturing and service sectors tend to be in urban areas, the trend is for increasing concentration and urbanisation, especially in the Third World, with large movements of people from rural to urban areas. Thus economic factors can have a very significant affect on population distributions.

3. Political factors

Political considerations can also have an important impact on population patterns. In the past, military considerations were very influential in altering population distributions, whereas today regional planning policies are significant.

(a) Military considerations

Often military considerations, both defensive and offensive, have determined population distribution. Even in areas where the need for military considerations has gone, settlement patterns still reflect past needs.

(i) *Defensive settlements*. The need to defend valuable resources, such as rich agricultural lands, minerals and communication routes, has influenced past population distributions. These patterns often persist into the modern landscape, although the need for defence has disappeared. In Northumberland, the threat of incursions from the north during the Middle Ages and Tudor period, meant that farming communities developed in defensible villages. The village of Warkworth provides an excellent example of this. The village is sited in a meander of the River Coquet, and is thus protected on three sides by the river, with a large Norman castle sited at the neck of the meander. Today 1300 people live in the village, and although the castle is now in ruins, the medieval pattern of land holding consisting of long thin *burgage* plots is still very much in evidence, as can be seen in Plate 1.3.

Newcastle-upon-Tyne represents a settlement which was developed under Roman occupation to protect the crossing point of the River Tyne. Since then Newcastle has grown and flourished as both a port, originally associated with the export of coal from the nearby coalfield, and as an industrial centre, involved principally with heavy engineering and ship building. Despite the fact that the city is now bypassed by road traffic, Newcastle has a population of 280 000, and is the capital of North East England, with both an industrial and a service function.

Defence can take many forms. In flat areas such as The Netherlands, moats or canals formed important defensive elements of the landscape. Large walls or barriers were also popular defensive structures found in all cultures. Some people even built underground cities to which they could retreat for many months, in times of attack. This was the case in the early Christian period in Cappodocia in present-day Turkey.

Defensive considerations have been important factors in affecting population distributions in all parts of the old world. Many settlements today are relics of less stable periods of history.

(ii) *Offensive factors*. The need for protection has not been the only military consideration to influence settlement patterns. The need to subdue conquered peoples has also been important. For example, in the eighteenth century General Wade built a series of military roads and garrison towns in the Highlands of Scotland. Fort William, which has developed from one of these garrison towns, is now an important town with a distillery, paper mill and aluminium smelting plant, as well as being a tourist centre. In the overseas colonies many garrison towns were established to impose colonial rule, and although they have now lost their military function, they still attract investment and population.

(b) Government policies

Government policies concerning the distribution and growth of populations are very significant. So important are these policies, especially in the twentieth century,

Plate 1.3 This aerial view of the village of Warkworth in Northumberland shows the village's superb defensive situation. Note the castle and the bridge over the River Coquet. The long thin burgage plots inherited from the Middle Ages still dominate the pattern of land ownership. (Photograph: Air Fotos)

Plate 1.4   These ornate walls are part of the defences of the city of Jaipur in India. Today they provide shelter for street traders. (Photograph: G. O'Hare)

Plate 1.5   Hill-tops were often chosen as defensive sites for settlements. This village in the Atlas Mountains of Morocco provides an excellent example of this type of situation. (Photograph: H.R. Barrett)

that they are now recognised as major demographic factors. These policies are dealt with in detail in Chapter 6.

ASSIGNMENTS

1. (a) Using a good atlas compare the global distribution of the following factors with population, shown in Figure 1.1:
    i) physical features such as mountains, deserts and deltas;
    ii) rainfall (or agricultural growing season);
    iii) soil types.
  (b) Discuss any patterns identified and suggest reasons for them.

2. *Study past records of the settlement you live in. These can be found in your*
   local history library (or museum) or in a good local history textbook.
   (a) By analysing old maps, diagrams and census reports, describe the
      population history of your settlement.
   (b) Identify the main factors that have contributed to the growth (or decline) of
      the settlement.
   (c) What is the present function of the settlement? How has this changed
      through time? What effect has this had on population numbers?
   (d) How significant are the factors described in this section, in explaining the
      population history of the settlement?
3. *In what ways may improvements in the following technologies affect population*
   growth and distribution:
   (a) agriculture;
   (b) industry;
   (c) transport/communications;
   (d) domestic;
   (e) medical?

D. Population and Carrying Capacity

The relationship between population and resources, particularly food, has been a focus of concern for thousands of years, and periodic famine was a fact of life for many peoples. The delicate balance between population numbers and food supplies has again been highlighted in the 1970s and 1980s with the well-documented famines in the Horn of Africa and the Sahel.

During the 1950s and 1960s grain production exceeded population growth on every continent. But in the early 1970s production in Africa fell below population growth and in the 1980s the same situation occurred in Latin America. In 1988 Africa imported a total of 28 million tonnes of grain to feed the population, whilst Latin America imported 11 million tonnes. This is in stark contrast to Western Europe which since 1950 has become a net exporter of grain, second only to USA. As a result, the debate continues.

1. Malthusian gloom

(a) Malthus' predictions

The notion that environments are finite and can sustain only a given number of people is not new. Almost two hundred years ago a British economist, Thomas Malthus, published a very influential paper entitled, *Essay on the principle of population* (1798). In this essay Malthus investigated the relationship between population and food supply. He argued that population, when left unchecked, increased geometrically, i.e. 2, 4, 8, 16 etc, whereas subsistence or food supplies increased only arithmetically, i.e. 1, 2, 3, 4 and so on. The inevitable result would

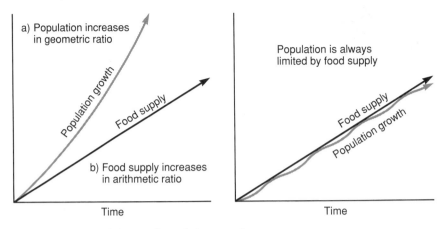

Figure 1.6   Malthus' theory of population growth

be that at some point in time population numbers would exceed the amount of food available and population would always be constrained by food supply (see Figure 1.6). When this occurred Malthus argued that population growth would have to be reduced to maintain the balance. This he concluded would take place by the implementation of a series of what he called positive and preventative checks. Malthus defined the positive checks to population growth as misery (which included famine, disease and war) and vice (which embraced abortion, sexual perversion and infanticide). The preventative checks to population growth were exemplified by moral restraint, and included sexual abstinence and late marriage.

Malthus' fundamental thesis that population growth would be curtailed by insufficient food supplies was largely ignored until fairly recently. The demographic and economic history of Europe in the nineteenth and early twentieth centuries seemed to disprove him. Population had continued to grow and yet there had been no major global natural shortage of food-stuffs. Malthus' prediction had in fact been postponed by the discovery of the new worlds such as North America and Australasia, which absorbed surplus population and produced excess food, the harnessing of fossil fuels and the implementation of technological innovations which increased agricultural production. However, by the 1960s and 1970s the balance between population growth and resources had become critical once more, with well publicised incidents of regional famine and increasing desertification. Once again scientists began to ask the Malthusian question: is there a limit to population growth?

(b) Limits to growth

Following evidence that world population was growing at a much faster rate during the 1960s than had been predicted, a number of alarmist books appeared. Popular paperback editions included *The population bomb*, (1968) by P. Erlich and *Only one earth*, (1972) by B. Ward and R. Dubos. These books predicted catastrophe for the world if population growth was not slowed down. The debate heightened in

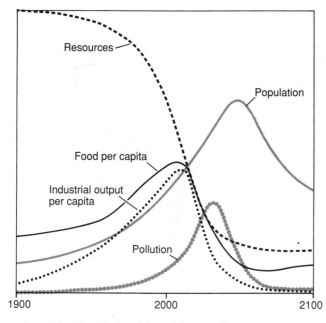

The "standard" world model run assumes no major change in the physical, economic, or social relationships that have historically governed the development of the world system. All variables plotted here follow historical values from 1900 to 1970. Food, industrial output, and population grow exponentially until the rapidly diminishing resource base forces a slowdown in industrial growth. Because of natural delays in the system, both population and pollution continue to increase for some time after the peak of industrialisation. Population growth is finally halted by a rise in the death rate due to decreased food and medical services.

Figure 1.7   The Limits of Growth 'standard' computer run (Source: Meadows *et al*, 1972)

1972 with the publication of the highly influential, but now largely discredited, Club of Rome report entitled, *The limits to growth*. This report was based on a series of computer models which simulated the global interaction of five basic factors, population growth, non-renewable resources, agricultural output, industrial output and pollution. These factors, it was suggested, would ultimately limit population growth. Computer runs were made projecting current facts and trends into the future, using a number of different scenarios. Figure 1.7 shows the standard run of the model, using the five factors, which assumed that non-renewable resources would last for 250 years (at 1970 usage rates). The system collapses well before the year 2100. The conclusion of the team was that if population growth was not to be limited by natural factors, then self-imposed limitation of births (as occurred in China in the 1980s) must take place, accompanied by a shift in emphasis from industry to agriculture and the adoption of *environmentally friendly*, i.e. pollution-free, life styles.

   Although the assumptions of the model were eventually much criticised, along with the poor quality of the available data and its lack of socio-political content, the report demonstrated scientifically the concerns expressed by Malthus two centuries earlier. It also broadened the Malthusian argument, incorporating environmental issues into the debate.

(c) Carrying capacity

The essential debate concerning population growth and its relationship with resources and the environment has been greatly advanced by the development of ecological ideas, and particularly the concept of 'carrying capacity'. This concept has long been used by biologists and ecologists, but has only recently been recognised by population geographers as a useful tool. The carrying capacity of a natural system can be expressed in terms of the maximum number of organisms that can be sustained by the food producing system without impairing the ability of that system to continue producing. If the numbers of organisms depending on a biological system become excessive, then the system will slowly be destroyed. For example, when an area of ocean is overfished, stocks dwindle and the fishery will collapse; similarly, when forest cutting exceeds regrowth, forest cover will consequently decrease. The same concept can be applied to human populations.

Figure 1.8 demonstrates the possible consequences for a human population when carrying capacity is exceeded. As shown in Figure 1.8a, population overshoots the carrying capacity of the environment (or the ability of the environment to support them) and adjustment of the population takes place with the previously existing equilibrium being restored. In Figure 1.8b carrying capacity is exceeded but the human population continues to expand, consuming the biological resource itself. The result is that human consumption and numbers have to be reduced as the biological system collapses. In Figure 1.8c population expands but impending disaster is postponed by the application of technologies that raise the carrying capacity of the life support system.

The concept of carrying capacity is particularly useful to population geographers when considering the concept of overpopulation. It helps explain why some areas with low population densities, such as Africa with on average only 18 persons per square kilometre, are believed to be overpopulated, while others, such as Western Europe, with a much higher population density of 155 persons per square kilometre,

Plate 1.6   The use of irrigation technology can increase the carrying capacity of an area. This traditional water wheel in Morocco enables an otherwise semi-arid environment to support olive groves. (Photograph: H.R. Barrett)

a) Population stabilises at maximum carrying capacity

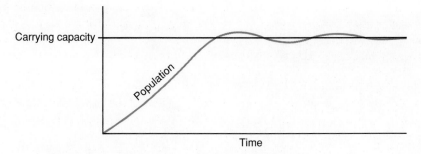

b) Population growth exceeds carrying capacity and biological
resource base is destroyed, as a result population decreases

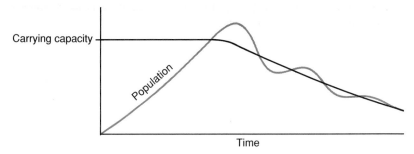

c) Population growth exceeds carrying capacity, which
is increased to accommodate population growth

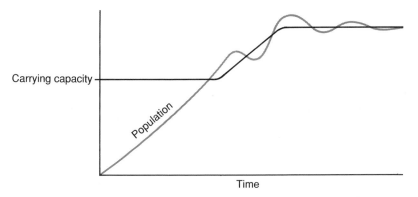

Figure 1.8   Relationship between population growth and carrying capacity

are not. The important point is that carrying capacities are not fixed through time.
They are a function of technology and can therefore be raised or lowered. It is the
level of economic development and technological application that will determine a
region's human carrying capacity. The optimal number of people that a biological
system can support without degradation is known as the *sustainable population.*

25

Plate 1.7   Irrigation allows crops to be grown all year round in semi-arid and arid regions. This modern irrigation scheme, near Larache in Morocco, enables sugar cane to be cultivated as a cash crop, in an otherwise unsuitable area. (Photograph: H.R. Barrett)

Once this number has been exceeded the life support system of the area will slowly be destroyed if actions are not taken to increase the carrying capacity of the region or to reduce population numbers.

As an analytical tool, carrying capacity is becoming increasingly popular in the identification of general relationships between population pressure and resources under specific economic systems. The practical application of this concept is demonstrated in the case study of the West African Sahel at the end of this chapter. But carrying capacities in many parts of the world are not easy to assess, due to lack of data and difficulties in devising a universal method of calculation: instead they are usually derived from estimates. Nevertheless without this concept the term 'overpopulation' becomes a subjective value judgement.

In many instances, population pressure can be blamed for the disruption of life support systems. However, the concept of carrying capacity illustrates the fact that reducing population growth itself is often only one part of a two-way solution. In many regions the resource base on which a population depends can be raised through the investment of capital and technology and the importation of energy. Investment in modern inputs can dramatically raise the population carrying capacity of croplands, although this is very often dependent on technological breakthroughs such as genetically engineered, high-yielding crop varieties.

2. Technological hope

Boserup's thesis

One of the major criticisms of the Malthusian thesis is that at a global level catastrophe has not occurred, although at a local and regional level there are examples of such disasters, especially in the less developed regions, for example Bangladesh and Ethiopia. It is argued that scientific and technological innovation decoupled the world from the Malthusian dilemma, particularly in the developed world. One of the first persons to articulate this argument was Esther Boserup, who in 1965 published her highly influential book *Conditions of agricultural growth*. Boserup argues that as population densities increase, human populations are forced to change their methods of food production and supply. When this occurs the carrying capacity of the region is increased and a Malthusian disaster is averted. Such increases in food production are always accompanied by technological innovation, for example irrigation, mechanisation and the use of chemical fertilisers. Social change may also ensue within the new production system.

According to Boserup, technological change is not a random occurrence, but is a response to population pressure. As a consequence, human history can be viewed as a long series of technological changes which have allowed, but also been the result of, population expansion. In the twentieth century technological innovations associated with birth control and agricultural production have meant that population increase has slowed and the production of resources has continued to expand, especially in the developed world.

3. Ecological concern

The technological solution to population problems, expounded by Boserup, has been widely criticised because it does not take into account the finite nature of non-renewable resources and the impact of waste products on the global system. The generation of environmental pollution intimated in the 1972 *Limits to growth* study have received large amounts of media attention in the late 1980s. It is now recognised that waste products which are released into the environment as a result of agricultural intensification and industrialisation not only damage the environment, but also harm people. The long-term effects on populations which are exposed to thousands of chemicals applied to fields, pollutants emitted from factories and waste products dumped on land and in the sea are largely unknown. This is because any deterioration of health due to pollutants may be delayed for many years and can be complicated by other factors. However, fatalities do take place as a direct result of pollution. At Minamata Bay, Japan, in the 1950s, for example, over 700 people died as a result of eating mercury-contaminated seafood. In the USA it is estimated that air pollution is responsible for 50 000 premature deaths each year. In 1984, in the world's biggest industrial disaster, over 2500 people died as a direct result of inhaling toxic gas escaping from a chemical pesticide plant in Bhophal, India. Nuclear accidents also threaten human life. In 1986, thirty people died as a direct result of the Chernobyl nuclear disaster in USSR; but the number that will die prematurely as a result of that accident is estimated to be tens of thousands. Though the consequences of pollution on human health are difficult to measure, pressure is increasingly being put on governments by a worried general public to control harmful emissions.

Many of the instances described above are local in their effect, but the increased emissions of carbon dioxide into the atmosphere may have a more global impact. Many scientists now believe that the world is getting warmer. Such global warming may be predominantly the result of increased emissions of carbon dioxide, methane, chloroflourocarbons (CFCs) and water vapour, and is commonly known as the

Plate 1.8   Fire crews fight the burning chemical plant at Flixborough, near Scunthorpe, which exploded in 1974. The explosion, which occurred on a Saturday when only maintenance work was being undertaken, killed 30 people and injured one hundred. (Photograph: Popperfoto)

greenhouse effect. Such a phenomenon may affect human health directly, but could also affect food production, and ultimately reduce global carrying capacities.

There is a great deal of discussion and speculation as to the probable affect of global warming on the earth. Most computer models predict a reduction in the polar ice caps and a thermal expansion of the oceans which will produce a global rise in sea levels. At the same time there will also be a disruption of rainfall patterns. Rainfall predictions such as that shown in Figure 1.9 suggest that continental interiors will become drier while coasts will become wetter, with mid-latitudes experiencing higher levels of precipitation and low-middle latitudes (about 40°N) receiving less. This has serious implications for global food security since it means that the grain producing regions of North America and USSR (about 40°N) are projected to receive reduced rainfall. However, warmer climates may open vast tracts of land to agricultural production in Canada, northern Europe and USSR.

Not only will rainfall changes affect agricultural patterns, but sea level rise may threaten large areas of agricultural lowland. Current predictions intimate that during the next 40 years sea levels will rise by possibly 20–40 cm. Storms combined with a high tide in these circumstances may breach or exceed existing sea defences, causing floods similar to that affecting The Netherlands and East Anglia in 1953. The developed countries such as UK, The Netherlands and USA will probably be able to cope by improving their sea defences, but poor countries such as Bangladesh and Egypt may find large areas of their present land area permanently under water. Not only will valuable rice lands located on flood and coastal plains be damaged permanently, with salt intrusion and flooding, but thousands of people may lose their homes, if not their lives. It is estimated, for example, that 300 000 islanders in the South Pacific and Indian Oceans alone would have to abandon their homes if sea level rose by 50 cm, and many of the world's major cities would be subject to

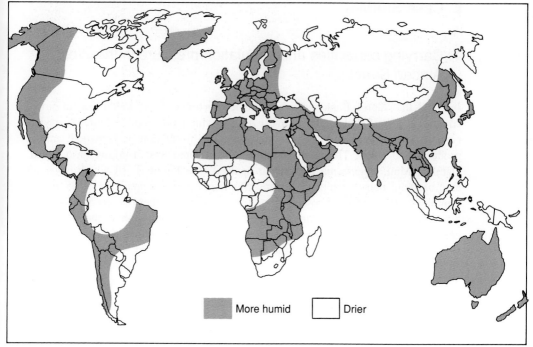

Figure 1.9   Possible climatic consequences of a 1 °C rise in global temperature (Source:
V.R.O. Kartografische Verlagsgesellschaft mbH, 1986)

annual flooding, including London, Venice, Bangkok, Alexandria, New York, Tokyo,
and Buenos Aires, affecting millions of urban dwellers. If, as a result of air pollution,
the world is getting warmer, then human populations all over the globe will be
affected. Adaptation to sea level rise and changing rainfall patterns will be inevitable
and necessary.

ASSIGNMENTS

1. *(a) How might carrying capacities be raised in the following types of economy:*
    i) subsistence based on agricultural production;
    ii) mineral based;
    iii) industrial, principally manufacturing?
   *(b) What might be the environmental impact of the solutions you have put
       forward?*
   (c) How would population numbers be affected?
2. *Choose a recognised environmental problem. This could be global, regional or
   even a local issue. Using journals, TV and press reports:*
   (a) describe the ecological problem.
   (b) what is or may be the impact on human populations?
   (c) how can the problem be solved?
3. *'Boserup's hypothesis does not disprove Malthus' predictions, it just delays
   them.' Discuss this statement using examples.*

29

E. Case Studies

1. Carrying capacities and population pressure in the West African Sahel

In 1987 the World Bank published the results of a study undertaken in seven countries of the Sahel region in West Africa, which assessed the human carrying capacity of the region in terms of its biological production of fuelwood, animal products and crops. The seven countries investigated were Burkina Faso, Chad, Gambia, Mali, Mauritania, Niger and Senegal (see Figure 1.10) which cover an area of more than 5.3 million square kilometres. It is an area where the annual rainfall is low, ranging from less than 200 mm in the northern desert areas to over 800 mm further south. Precipitation does not fall evenly throughout the year but is concentrated into a short summer rainy season, which is approximately one month long in the north of the region and can be up to five months long further south. More important than total rainfall is the number of months in which precipitation exceeds potential evapotranspiration, thus determining the length of the growing season. As Figure 1.11 demonstrates, this again follows a north-south progression, with the growing season being less than one month in the north, and increasing to six months in the southern areas of the region. Because of the importance of the climatic regime to the area, ecological zones are frequently determined by levels of available moisture. The World Bank has identified five zones using rainfall as the criteria. These are shown in Figure 1.12 and represent ecological bands running

Figure 1.10   Countries of the West African Sahel

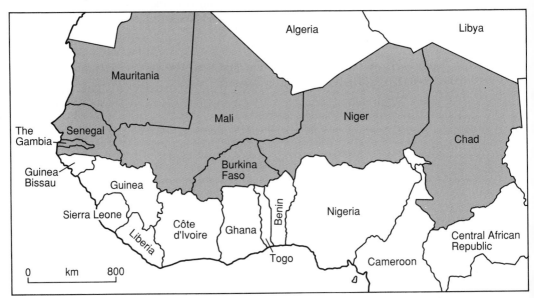

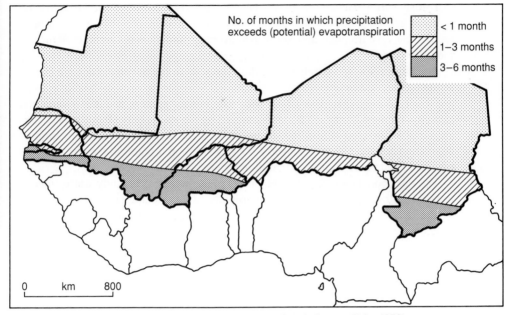

Figure 1.11   Rainfall effectiveness in the West African Sahel (Source: Udo, 1978)

Figure 1.12   Rainfall zones in the West African Sahel

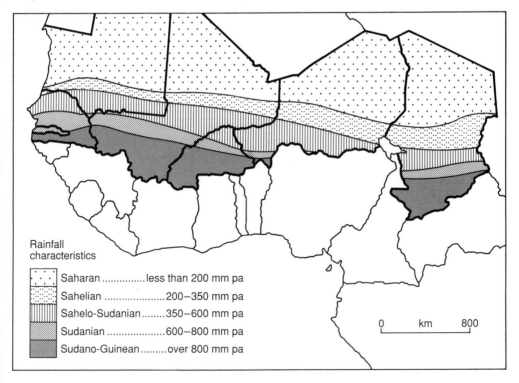

31

east-west across the region. It can be seen that two-thirds of the study region receives less than 200 mm of rainfall annually. In recent years the area has been typified by very irregular and lower than average rainfall, resulting in drought and food shortages.

Apart from low and unreliable rainfall, the soils in the Sahelian zone are of low fertility. They are deficient in phosphates and nitrogen, as well as having a weak and easily disaggregated structure with low humus content and water retention capacity. Of the 530 million hectares covered by the study, only 60 million hectares are suitable for crop cultivation, of which 20% lie between the northern limit of cultivation and the 350 mm isohyet. About 150 million hectares of the area supports rangeland and the remaining 320 million hectares are unproductive.

The total population of the seven countries included in the study was estimated to be 31 million. Overall densities are low, the average being only six persons per square kilometre for the entire area. However, densities can reach 100 persons per square kilometre in places. The lowest national density of 1.5 is found in Mauritania and the highest of 60 has been recorded for The Gambia. Population growth rates are high, standing at approximately 3% per annum. On this calculation the area will have 75% more people to support by the year 2000, reaching a population total of 54 million, in comparison to a population of 19 million in 1961. Within the region population is remarkably unevenly distributed, with over 80% of the population living in 25% of the total area. Over 40% of the population is concentrated in the more humid Sahelo-Sudanic zone which comprises only 10% of the total area.

The seven countries of this study comprise some of the poorest nations in the world. None of the countries had a GNP *per capita in* 1986 of more than $420 (compared with $8870 for the UK). Senegal and Mauritania had the highest GNP *per capita* of $420 whereas Burkina Faso had the lowest at $150. Poverty and the low government priority given to subsistence agriculture in the past has meant that the region is dominated by productive systems that are traditional in character. These are systems developed by local residents over long periods of time which are essentially subsistence in nature. These systems are characterised by high labour and animal inputs and few modern technologies such as high-yielding seeds, irrigation equipment or chemical fertilisers. Within the household the main energy supply for cooking is derived from fuelwood collected locally, very little energy being imported into this region. As a result of such energy restraints the carrying capacity of the region is low. The World Bank calculates that based on traditional agriculture and livestock systems the sustainable population of the region is 36 million, as compared to a total population in 1980 of 31 million, giving a surplus capacity of only five million. However, the sustainable population calculated for fuelwood collected from the natural forest cover is only 21 million, demonstrating that in 1980 the biological system was already under severe stress.

The results of the study are shown in Table 1.3. In all zones the carrying capacity of the natural forest cover is lower than for crops and livestock and is therefore the most vulnerable part of the ecosystem. In four of the five zones actual population already exceeds the sustainable population of the natural forest cover.

Table 1.3 Estimates of sustainable human populations for crops, livestock and fuelwood in the West African Sahel (Source: compiled from Gorse & Steeds, 1987)

	Rainfall	Area		Population			Sustainable Population (millions)					
		ha '000s	%	density per km²	%	millions	crops	livestock	total food	population food disparity	fuel-wood	population fuelwood disparity
Saharan	less than 200 mm	3520	67	0.5	5.7	1.8	0	1.0	1.0	−0.8	0.2	−1.6
Sahelian	200–350 mm	450	8	9	13	4.0	2.8	1.1	3.9	−0.1	0.3	−3.7
Sahelo-Sudanian	350–600 mm	550	10	24	42.2	13.1	6.0	2.7	8.7	−4.4	6.0	−7.1
Sudanian	600–800 mm	380	7	21	26.1	8.1	6.4	2.5	8.9	+0.8	7.4	−0.7
Sudano-Guinean	over 800 mm	400	8	10	13	4.0	10.0	3.8	13.8	+8.8	7.1	+3.1
Totals		5300	100	6	100	31.0	25.2	11.1	36.3	+4.3	21.0	−10.1

Plate 1.9   As land degradation and deforestation increase, women, the main porters of domestic water and fuelwood, have to walk further to collect these valuable resources. Here in Burkina Faso (West Africa) women walk long distances through parched landscapes to collect water. Notice the traditional earthenware pots and buckets made from discarded inner tubes, which are used to transport the water. (Photograph: Ron Giling/Panos Pictures)

This means that in many parts of the region rapid deforestation is taking place, resulting in land degradation and desertification. It also means that women, who are generally responsible for fuelwood collection, are spending more and more time and energy finding supplies of fuelwood. This is time and energy which could be put to more productive use, either in the home or on the farm. In terms of food production, carrying capacity is marginally exceeded in two zones, but exceeded by a much larger proportion in the Sahelo-Sudanian zone due to the large number of people living there. By contrast in the Sudano-Guinean zone, the actual population is much lower than the potentially sustainable population.

When the data in Table 1.3 is studied it becomes clear that the Sahelian, and more particularly the Sahelo-Sudanian, zone is suffering great environmental stress due to population pressure. These two zones are therefore vulnerable to the desertification process. This study, by employing the concept of carrying capacity, clearly demonstrates that environmental stress and population pressure is occurring in the Sahelo-Sudanian belt, and it is in this zone that efforts to raise carrying capacity or reduce population numbers should be concentrated.

It is clear that current population growth rates in the West African Sahelian region cannot be sustained for very much longer without a deterioration in living standards. The balance between population and the life support system must be redressed. This can be achieved by intensifying food production through irrigation projects or by developing non-rural employment opportunities as well as the adoption of family planning policies and the possible implementation of projects to resettle people into the Sudano-Guinean zone. Other solutions include afforestation schemes, the introduction of more energy-efficient cooking stoves and the use of other domestically produced fuels. But all these solutions require capital investment which these countries do not have. The future for people living in the Sahelian region of West Africa does not seem to offer much potential or hope.

2. Projected global sea level rise and its impact on Bangladesh

Most scientists agree that global warming is presently taking place, caused by the accumulation of *greenhouse gases*. Among the disruptions expected from global warming is the thermal expansion of the seas, resulting in rising sea levels. The United Nations estimate is that sea levels may rise by over one metre in the next 50-60 years. As a result many nations are expected to require coastal and estuarine defences, and many populous cities will be threatened. In the developed world measures are already being taken to protect cities, with the implementation of projects such as the Thames Barrage to protect London (see Plate 1.10). However, the impact of global sea level rise is difficult to predict because of local geological processes such as tectonic lift and coastal subsidence.

Apart from inundation the other anticipated effects of sea level rise are accelerated coastal erosion, damage to drainage and irrigation systems and saline intrusion into groundwater, rivers and farmland. As half of the world's population lives in coastal regions, the expected impact of sea level rise on human populations is extremely serious, particularly for the poorer nations where, due to the excessive cost of building sea defences, valuable agricultural land may be destroyed or lost.

Bangladesh, with a GNP *per capita* of $160 in 1986 and an average population density of 685 people per square kilometre in 1985, is one of the poorest and most

Plate 1.10   The Thames Barrier which was finished in 1984 is designed to protect London from tide surges. This view of the Barrier is taken from the south side of the river looking upstream. (Photograph: R.E. Pearson)

densely populated countries in the world (see Figure 1.13). Geologically, Bangladesh comprises part of the Bengal Basin and apart from the Chittagong Hills near the Burmese border, is made up of recent alluvial deposits transported by the three great rivers, the Brahmaputra, Ganges and Meghna, that flow through the country into the Bay of Bengal. Figure 1.14 shows that Bangladesh, with an area of 144 000 square kilometres, is a deltaic land where over 80% of the country is classified as flood plain and 40% of the country is less than one metre above sea level. Because of its poverty, high population (100 million in 1985) and topography the threat to the country from sea level rise is a real and very serious one.

Flooding is very much part of the normal cycle of the seasons in Bangladesh. The formation of the delta relies on flooding and much of the country's fertility can

Figure 1.13   Population density of Bangladesh, 1981 (Source: Johnson, 1982)

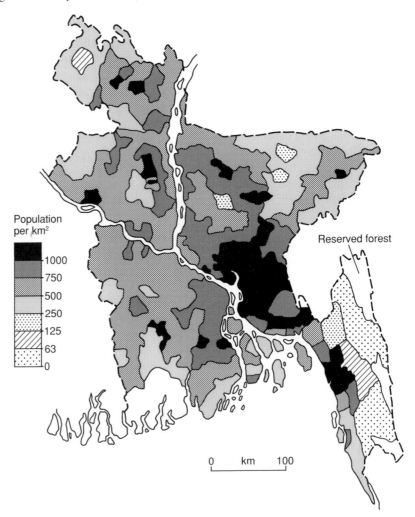

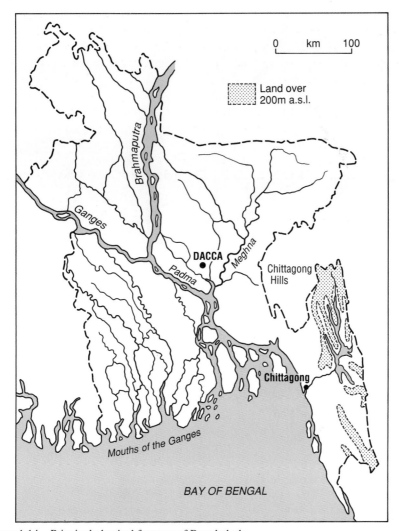

Figure 1.14   Principal physical features of Bangladesh

be attributed to nutrients contained in the flood waters that affect the country during the June to September monsoon period. The area prone to flooding is shown in Figure 1.15. This map shows that over 50% of the country is vulnerable to flooding and that over a third of the land area experiences floods annually. In the years since independence from Pakistan in 1971, Bangladesh has experienced six devastating floods (1971, 1974, 1978, 1984, 1987, 1991), all resulting in loss of life and economic devastation. In 1987 more than 24 million people, that is 20% of the population, were displaced and over 700 people died after some of the worst floods in the region's history. Although the loss of life was low in this instance, the government estimated that 2 million tonnes of grain had been lost and more than 25 000 cattle killed. Predicted sea level rise will undoubtedly compound the already

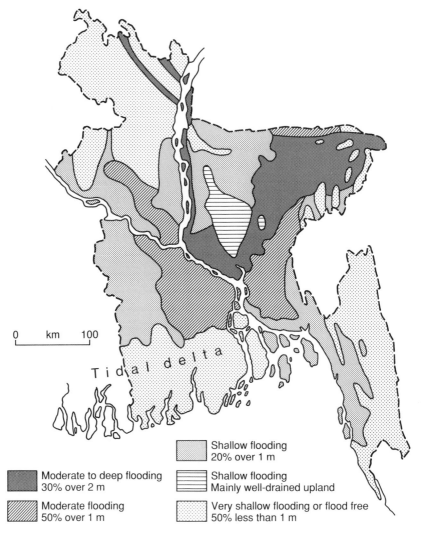

Figure 1.15 Severity of flooding in Bangladesh (Source: Johnson, 1982)

serious inundation problems experienced by the country. The flooding of 1991, associated with a cyclone, resulted in an estimated 200 000 deaths and widespread destruction.

The severity of the effect of sea level rise on Bangladesh will depend on the interaction between global sea level rise and local land subsidence. Although the country faces problems of excess supplies of water in the monsoon period, for the rest of the year there is a water deficit. This, combined with growing population pressure and the need to grow more food has resulted in the increased withdrawal of groundwater for irrigation, which directly affects subsidence rates. If the extraction

Plate 1.11 Flooding has become an accepted part of life in Bangladesh. Here in the capital, Dacca, despite deep flooding, life goes on. (Photograph: Shanidul Alam/Panos Pictures)

Plate 1.12 For the poor of Bangladesh, flooding may mean the loss of everything. In this picture a woman and her two children shelter in their home with their belongings, waiting for the water to subside. (Photograph: Shanidul Alam/Panos Pictures)

of groundwater increases, it is likely that subsidence will also increase, with the result that the impact of any global sea level rise will be greater.

A recent study has predicted two possible outcomes of sea level rise on Bangladesh, shown in Table 1.4. Both scenarios assume a global sea level rise of 0.79 metres by 2050 increasing to 2.17 by 2100. They differ, however, in their assessment of the impact of local land subsidence. Scenario 1 assumes local land subsidence will be 0.65 metres by 2050 and 1.15 metres by 2100; scenario 2 is based upon land subsidence estimates of double these figures. Under scenario 1 a predicted local rise in sea level of 1.44 metres by the year 2050 would mean that 16% of habitable land would be under water and 13% of the population would be displaced. Under the same scenario, 27% of the Bangladeshi population would have to be relocated by the year 2100. If the rate of local land subsidence is doubled, as in scenario 2, then the number of people displaced by the year 2100 would be over 35% of the population, with over a third of the country's present land area lost to the sea. The social and economic effects of such a scenario would be devastating to the region, making it less likely to be able to protect its land and people from the sea. It is clear that the inevitable result of global warming on Bangladesh will be a reduction in carrying capacity.

Although Bangladesh is unlikely to influence global emissions of greenhouse gases, it can help to protect itself from sea level rise by reducing the pumping of groundwater and the erection of sea defences. This will be expensive. It is estimated, for example, that the Dutch will have to spend over $5 billion by the year 2040 just to maintain their coastal defences. A country as poor as Bangladesh is unlikely to be able to afford to protect its people in the same way. It seems probable therefore that by the year 2100, Bangladesh as it is known today will cease to exist. Bangladesh will be only one of the victims of a problem created in the developed world.

ASSIGNMENTS

1. (a) *Using Table 1.3 and Figure 1.12 as an outline, plot the following:*
    i) *population density of the five rainfall zones;*
    ii) *population/food disparity of the five rainfall zones;*
    iii) *population/fuelwood disparity of the five rainfall zones.*
   (b) *Describe the patterns you have plotted.*
   (c) *What are the implications of the data for future population growth and distribution in the various rainfall zones of the region?*
   (d) *Comment on the usefulness of the concept of carrying capacity when considering population densities.*
2. (a) *Using a good atlas, select one of the following countries:*
    i) *Egypt;*
    ii) *The Gambia;*
    iii) *Mexico;*
    and comment on the environmental impact of a 1.5 metre rise in sea level.
   (b) *Estimate the proportion of the population that would be displaced by such an event.*
   (c) *Compare your findings with the predicted impact on Bangladesh (see Table 1.4).*

Table 1.4   The effects of sea level rise on Bangladesh (Source: adapted from Brown, 1989)

		Global sea level rise (metres)	Local land subsidence (metres)	Local sea level rise* (metres)	Habitable land lost %	Population displaced %
Scenario 1	2050	0.79	0.65	1.44	16	13
	2100	2.17	1.15	3.32	26	27
Scenario 2	2050	0.79	1.30	2.09	18	15
	2100	2.17	2.30	4.47	34	35

* Includes global sea level rise and local land subsidence

Key Ideas

Introduction

1. Population geography is the study of spatial variations in the distribution, composition, migration and growth of populations.
2. Population geography is distinguished from demography by its concern with spatial patterns.
3. Population geographers are concerned not only with describing patterns and distributions, but also try to explain them.
4. The sub-discipline embraces almost every other aspect of geography and is regarded by many as the core of the wider discipline of geography.

A. Population distribution

1. People are unevenly distributed over the world's surface.
2. There are four major global concentrations of population: East Asia; South Asia; Europe; North-Eastern USA.
3. Three-quarters of the world's population lives within 1000 kilometres of the sea.

B. The process of population change

1. Population change in any region is the result of the balance between births and deaths, as well as in- and out-migrations.
2. Present-day population numbers and distributions are the result of past variations in these *dynamic components*: births, deaths and migrations.

C. Factors affecting population distribution

1. The over-riding factor affecting population distribution is the ability of people to make a satisfactory living.
2. Ecological factors, including climate, soils and water availability, can have both a limiting as well as enhancing effect on the distribution of human populations. They are, however, inextricably linked to economic factors, as many less hospitable areas can be settled if economically attractive enough.
3. Energy sources, especially coal, and mineral resources have exercised a powerful influence on population distribution and densities.
4. The more complex a society becomes, the less directly do physical factors influence population distributions. Technology, economic activity and social organisation are equally if not more important than physical factors in determining population distributions.
5. Based on population/resource ratios and technological levels, Ackerman has identified five basic population resource regions: European; American; Brazilian; India-China; and Arctic-Desert.

6. Political considerations, especially military needs and planning policies, are important factors in the consideration of past and present population distributions.

D. Population and carrying capacity

1. Recent droughts have emphasised the important relationship between population, resources and the environment.
2. The notion that population numbers are constrained by food supply was put forward by Malthus in 1798. He argued that population growth would be constrained by both positive and preventative checks.
3. A Malthusian disaster has been postponed by migration to new territories and the implementation of technological innovations in food production.
4. In 1972 Malthus' concerns were given scientific credibility in the *Limits to growth* report. This report used computer technology to stress the important relationship between people, resources and the environment.
5. The *Limits to growth* model was much criticised for its lack of socio-political content.
6. The debate concerning population, resources and ecology has been greatly enhanced by the concept of carrying capacity. This concept is particularly useful to population geographers when considering overpopulation.
7. Carrying capacities are determined by levels of economic development and technological application. It is difficult to evaluate them due to a lack of a universal method of calculation.
8. Boserup argues that Malthusian disaster is avoided because as population pressure increases technological innovation takes place, raising carrying capacity.
9. It is now recognised that pollution not only damages the environment but also harms people.
10. The human damage may be immediate but is more often long term and therefore difficult to evaluate.
11. Global warming and sea level rise present serious problems to many nations. In particular altered rainfall patterns and the loss of productive land and living space may reduce regional, and even the global, carrying capacity.

E. Case Studies

1. In the West African Sahel carrying capacity for fuelwood is exceeded in 92% of the area, and for food production is exceeded in 85% of the area.
2. The region is therefore suffering great environmental stress due to population pressure.
3. Sea level rise associated with global warming threatens populations, especially in poorer countries, as they can not afford sea defences.
4. Bangladesh is particularly vulnerable, since 40% of the country is less than one metre above sea level.

Table 1.5 Annual rate of change of food (crops and livestock) production in relation to population growth for 105 developing countries, 1974–1984 (Source: FAO, 1985)

Rate of change of food ouput (%)	Population Growth (%)						1984 Population (millions)
	1.5 and below	1.6 to 2.0	2.1 to 2.5	2.6 to 3.0	3.1 to 3.5	3.6 and above	
−3.0 and below	Trinidad and Tobaco					Saudi Arabia	11.9
−2.9 to −2.0			Lesotho		Ghana		14.5
−1.9 to 0.1	Kampuchea Dominica Puerto Rico		Gambia Yemen	Peru Namibia Nicaragua	Zimbabwe Zambia Senegal	Botswana Mozambique Guinea-Bissau	78.4
0.0 to 0.9	Jamaica	Mauritius Burundi	Cameroon Haiti Guyana Dem. Yemen Guinea	Bolivia Costa Rica	Angola		49.3
1.0 to 1.5	Gabon Uruguay Samoa Afghanistan	Sierra Leone	Central African Rep. Nepal Dominican Rep.	Madagascar Sudan Tunisia			84.6

1.6 to 2.0	Cyprus	Chile Barbados	Chad Burkina Faso	Zaire Egypt El Salvador	Morocco Uganda Algeria Ecuador Liberia	Kenya Somalia	203.3
2.1 to 2.5	Cape Verde	Reunion	Panama Congo Ethiopia Mali	Benin Papua New Guinea Togo	Venezuela		76.1
2.6 to 3.0	Korea Rep.	Argentina Bhutan	Turkey Colombia	Bangladesh Guatemala Malawi Mauritania	Iran Nigeria	Libya	403.3
3.1 to 3.5	Lebanon		India	Mexico	Tanzania Pakistan Paraguay		950.7
3.6 and above	China Cuba Suriname	Sri Lanka Indonesia	Brazil, Burma Korea, DPR Malaysia Thailand Vietnam	Niger Philippines Swaziland Jordan Lao	Rwanda Syria	Brunel Honduras Iraq Côte d' Ivoire	1655.0

Prod. > Population   Prod. = Population   Prod. < Population

45

5. A recent study predicts that 16-18% of Bangladesh will be lost by 2050, displacing 13-15% of the population.
6. Bangladesh will be only one victim of a problem created in the developed world.

Figure 1.16   Areas of UK which would be in danger of inundation in the year 2050, if sea level rose by five metres (predicted by Ark) (Source: Tooley, 1989)

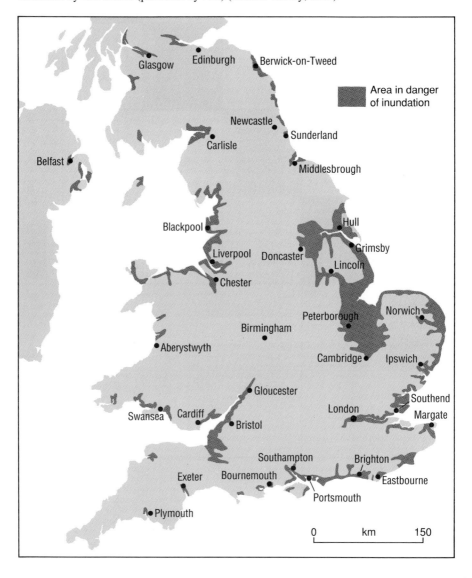

Additional Activities

1. (a) Study Table 1.5. Using the three categories of population/production relationships, draw a choropleth map of the data shown on Table 1.5. Describe the pattern shown.
   (b) Discuss the relationship between population output and population growth.
   (c) Do any of the theories and concepts discussed in Section D adequately explain the data?
2. (a) Using a good atlas, describe the population distribution of the UK.
   (b) Discuss to what extent ecological and mineral factors have affected the pattern described.
   (c) Figure 1.16 shows the areas of the UK which the environmental group Ark predicts will be in danger of inundation in 2050 if sea levels were to rise by five metres. Discuss the potential impact of such a rise on:
   i) population distribution;
   ii) agricultural production.
   (d) Assess the importance of ecological factors in determining population distributions.
3. Discuss the proposition that as technology advances, the influence of physical factors on population distribution declines.

2 The Demographic Transition

Introduction

In 1985 the world's population was estimated by the United Nations to be 4.8 billion, implying an annual rate of population increase of 1.7%. This represents an addition of 750 million people during the period 1975-85, a number equal to the estimated *total* world population living in 1750. According to the United Nations' calculations shown in Figure 2.1, additions to world population will average 86 million per year from 1990–95 and will reach a peak of 89 million each year between 1995 and 2000. After the year 2000, annual numbers will begin to decrease and the world's population will stabilise at approximately 10.2 billion by the end of the twenty-first century. This is a figure that is double the 1985 estimate.

The present-day global population is the result of two major surges in population growth. Before the eighteenth century, high global birth rates were matched by high death rates, ensuring that world population numbers grew very slowly. There were periods when regions experienced higher than average population growth but these were often counterbalanced by deaths caused by plagues and famines. However, at the beginning of the eighteenth century the first sustained increase in global population began. This was due to a decline in death rates which principally affected European populations and communities of Europeans living overseas in regions such as the Americas and Australia. It was an increase in European populations that lasted two hundred years. So great was this surge that the proportion of the world's population living in the developed world increased from an estimated 25% in 1750 to 34% in 1900.

The second surge in world population growth occurred after the Second World War, when population numbers increased dramatically in the less developed regions. It is a surge that, as Figure 2.1 shows, has dwarfed the European experience. Of the 2.3 billion added to the world's population between 1950 and 1985, those born in Asia accounted for 61%, with Africans and South Americans contributing 25%. This increase is the result of rapidly declining death rates in association with high birth rates. Africa, Asia and South America now contain 78% of the world's population, a figure that the United Nations estimate will rise to 86% by the end of the next century.

As discussed in Chapter 1, the relationship between birth rates, death rates and population change, in association with spatial and historical variations such as migrations, have long interested geographers. Although Malthus' work was well known, his ideas did not help in the analysis of population change and it was not until after the Second World War that an explanation was put forward.

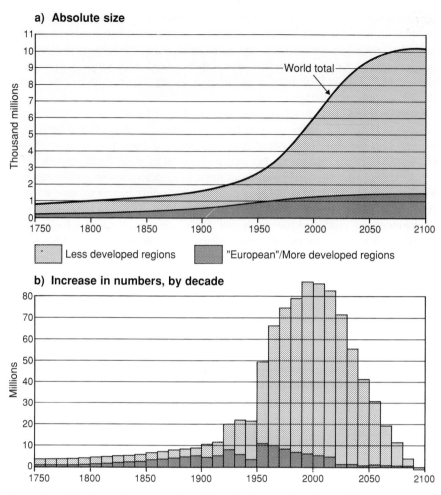

a) Absolute size

Less developed regions   "European"/More developed regions

b) Increase in numbers, by decade

Figure 2.1   World population growth, 1750–2100 (Source: Merrick, 1986)

A. The Demographic Transition Model

The notion of a demographic transition was first put forward by W.S. Thompson in 1929, but the theory did not take form until 1945 when F.W. Notestein presented the earliest statement of the model. He suggested that there was a relationship between population change and socio-economic development. He put forward three major postulates on which the model depended. The first was that decreases in mortality were the direct result of socio-economic change. Secondly he assumed that fertility was much less responsive to socio-economic changes, with decreases in fertility occurring some time after decreases in death rates. The inevitable implication was, therefore, that for a period of time birth rates would exceed death rates, resulting in increases in population numbers. Thirdly, Notestein believed that

49

socio-economic change took the form of an evolution from a traditional, non-industrial, usually agrarian society to a modern, industrial, urban society, a process which he termed *modernisation* and associated with Western-style economic development. The effect of such modernisation would be a drop in death rates followed by a drop in birth rates, resulting in a society experiencing a low natural increase, or static population.

Based on these three premises, Notestein put forward a four-stage model which is shown in Figure 2.2. Stage one consists of a period of high death and birth rates, resulting in a low but stable population. This stage is associated with traditional agricultural societies. However, as modernisation takes place death rates begin to decline (stage two). This decline in death rates, in association with continuing high birth rates, results in rapid population growth, which only begins to slow down in stage three, when birth rates also begin to decline. By stage four, economic development has produced low birth and death rates, resulting in a high, stable population living in an industrial urban society. Recently, however, a fifth stage of the model can be identified, a stage where low birth rates combined with rising death rates result in population decline (see Chapter 3).

As a population progresses through the demographic transition, the age and sex structure of its population will inevitably change. Population structure is the term used to describe the age and sex composition of a population and is often expressed visually as a population pyramid. In a population pyramid the number of males per age category are represented on the left hand side of the pyramid, with females on the right, as shown on Figure 2.3. The age structure of a population reflects its past pattern of demographic events, including mortality and migration, but more

Figure 2.2   The Demographic Transition Model

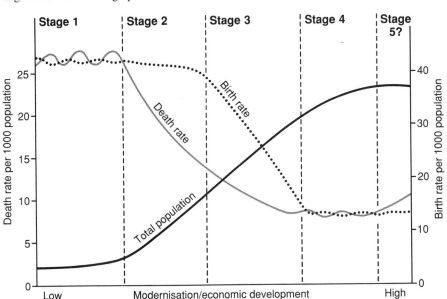

especially fertility, and can strongly influence future events. The proportion of children in the population will directly affect future population growth. So those countries with large bases to their pyramids will have a greater potential for population growth than those with smaller bases. In 1985, 37% of the people living in the less developed countries of the world were less than 15 years old, in comparison with 22% in the developed countries. This means that population will continue to grow in many parts of the Third World, even if couples have only two

Figure 2.3   Population pyramids of four countries at various stages of the Demographic Transition (Source: UN Demographic Yearbook, 1985)

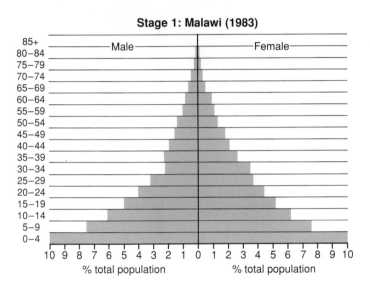

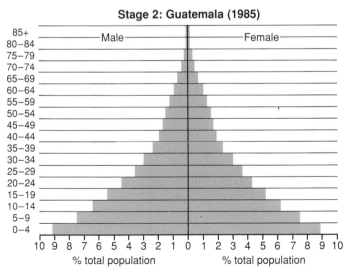

51

Stage 3: Thailand (1985)

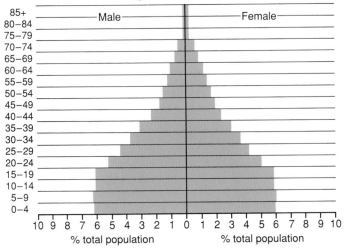

Stage 4: West Germany (1984)

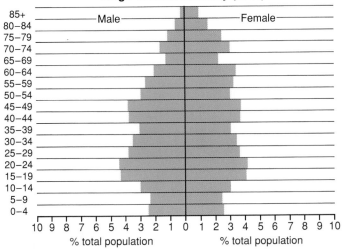

Fig. 2.3 (cont'd)

children. This phenomenon, known as *population momentum*, is the result of the generation which is producing births being disproportionately larger than the older generation, where most deaths occur. In the early stage of the demographic transition a large majority of the population will be young, as death rates are high. As death rates fall, but birth rates remain high (as in stages two and three of the demographic transition), the pyramid will contain a much higher proportion of children and hence a broader base (Figure 2.3). By stage four the pyramid is undergoing a reversal (Figure 2.3), with fewer children being born and a larger proportion of people surviving into old age.

Because of its influence on population size and structure, demographic transition theory has become very strongly associated with population geography and has become one of its major theoretical foundations. The model has been used by geographers in both a descriptive and a predictive capacity.

1. Demographic transition as descriptive model

As a descriptive model, the demographic transition seems to fit the experience of a number of countries very well, most notably UK and Sweden, and more recently Japan. Sweden has a longer record of vital statistics, which include births, deaths and marriages, than almost any other country. Due to its excellent demographic records Sweden is often used to demonstrate the descriptive accuracy of the model. When Swedish birth and death rates are plotted over time as in Figure 2.4, the similarity with the demographic transition model is striking. From 1750-1800 Sweden is typical of a country in stage one of the model, experiencing high birth and death rates, but after 1800 death rates begin to decline. There is an apparent 75-year time lag before birth rates begin to decrease and Sweden enters stage three of the model. By the 1970s birth and death rate decline has slowed down and the population has stabilised. By 1987, however, death rates have begun to rise and to exceed birth rates. Only time will show if this trend is to continue, with Sweden entering stage five of the model.

The pathway taken by a country when experiencing the demographic transition can be shown in graph form by plotting birth rates and death rates at specified time

Figure 2.4   Birth and death rates in Sweden, 1751–1987 (Source: adapted from Merrick, 1986; World Development Report, 1989)

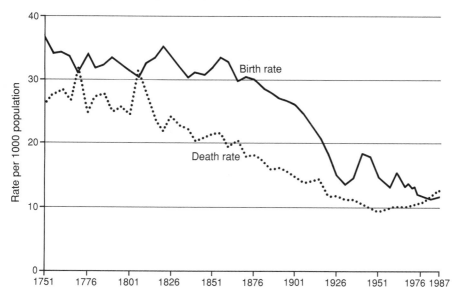

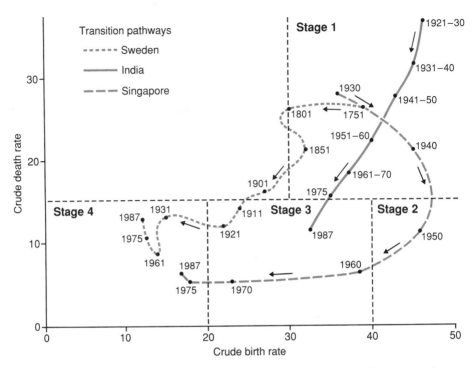

Figure 2.5 The Demographic Transition pathways traversed by India, Singapore and Sweden (Source: adapted from Heenan, 1980; World Development Report, 1989)

Figure 2.6 The position of twenty selected non-Islamic countries within the Demographic Transition, 1987 (Source: World Development Report, 1989)

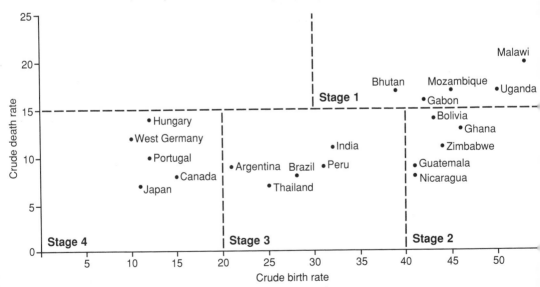

intervals. Figure 2.5 shows the pathway taken by Sweden, India and Singapore, and demonstrates that these countries are experiencing a demographic transition similar to that described above. The same graphical method can be used to locate and compare the transitional position of various countries at one point in time, as shown in Figure 2.6. Once located within the model, countries can be mapped according to their stage of demographic transition, and if this is done over time, a space-time diffusion of the transition can be identified. This was done in 1966 by R. Chung, who compiled ten maps for the period 1905-1960. From these maps he was able to trace the initial global diffusion of the demographic transition outwards from Western Europe, into Eastern Europe, Southern Europe, Anglo-America and Australasia. By the 1940s, the transition had spread to the USSR, the Caribbean, Latin America, South Africa and parts of Asia, and in the 1950s these regions were joined by Africa, the Middle East, China and South-east Asia. When Chung completed his study in 1960, stages two and three of the transition were occurring in Latin America, Asia, Africa, and the Middle East, with most mid-latitude countries in both the northern and southern hemispheres experiencing stage four of the model.

2. Demographic transition as predictive model

As a predictive model, the demographic transition model can be used to explain and therefore predict demographic change, as identified by Notestein. The model postulates that as economic development progresses (often measured by Gross National Product per capita), death rates will decline followed by birth rates, as happened in the West. However the model is open to criticism as there is no guarantee that Third World countries with very different cultural and economic experiences will follow this model.

When the birth rate and GNP per capita of various countries are examined (see Table 2.1) two major anomalies become apparent. First there are those countries with low GNP per capita and lower than expected birth rates, and secondly there are those countries with high GNP per capita, but higher than expected birth rates. The first group is rather varied, containing countries such as China, Sri Lanka and Thailand, all with strong government-supported family planning policies, as well as Poland and Hungary, where, until recently, the state played a central role in the economy. China, with 21% of the world's population, has one of the strictest and most publicised population policies in the world. Since 1979 the government has implemented a one-child-per-family policy, which has been very successful in reducing fertility and accounts for the country's very low birth rate, as compared with countries at a similar stage of economic development. However, the implications of the continuation of such a policy on the future age-structure of the Chinese population, has meant that the Chinese government is now relaxing its strict one-child policy. This example illustrates that government policy can be very influential indeed in determining birth rates. (See Chapter 6 for a fuller discussion of government population policies.) The second group of countries not fitting the model, includes those with a high GNP per capita and high birth rate. Countries

Table 2.1   Gross National Product (GNP) per capita and crude birth and death rates of 40 selected countries (Source: World Bank, 1989)

		(1987) GNP per capita $	CBR	CDR
1	Ethiopia	130	48	18
2	Bangladesh	160	41	15
3	Tanzania	180	50	14
4	Zambia	250	50	13
5	China	290	21	7
6	Togo	290	49	14
7	Kenya	330	52	11
8	Pakistan	350	47	12
9	Sri Lanka	400	23	6
10	Mauritania	440	48	19
11	Indonesia	450	29	9
12	Senegal	520	46	18
13	Morocco	610	35	10
14	Honduras	810	40	8
15	Thailand	850	25	7
16	Jamaica	940	26	6
17	Botswana	1 050	35	10
18	Peru	1 470	31	9
19	Syria	1 640	45	9
20	Malaysia	1 810	31	6
21	Poland	1 890	16	10
22	Brazil	2 020	28	8
23	Hungary	2 240	12	14
24	Argentina	2 390	21	9
25	Algeria	2 680	39	9
26	Portugal	2 830	12	10
27	Libya	5 460	44	9
28	Spain	6 010	12	9
29	Saudi Arabia	6 200	42	8
30	Singapore	7 940	17	6
31	UK	10 420	13	12
32	Belgium	11 480	12	12
33	W. Germany	14 400	10	12
34	Kuwait	14 610	33	3
35	Sweden	15 550	12	13
36	Japan	15 760	11	7
37	United Arab Emirates	15 830	23	4
38	Norway	17 190	13	11
39	USA	18 530	16	9
40	Switzerland	21 330	12	10

that belong to this group include Kuwait, Libya, Saudi Arabia and the United Arab Emirates. Unlike the previous group, these countries do have a common link in that they are all high-income oil exporters and embrace the Muslim culture. The relevance of the Demographic Transition Model to these countries will be examined in the case study at the end of this chapter.

The existence of such great anomalies has made many geographers question the validity of a model based on Western European experience that is applied to other cultural groups. Even within Europe the model breaks down, as in the case of France where fertility decline began long before industrialisation, and in the case of The Netherlands, where population increase in the nineteenth century was the result of increased fertility rather than declining mortality. Investigations into the factors that affect birth and death rates, such as population planning policies, public health programmes and religious culture, as outlined in Chapters 3 and 4, confirm that the model is over-simplified.

Although the model has been developed in several ways since 1945, the emphasis on economic forces to explain population change has remained. The neglect of cultural factors is a serious shortcoming of the model. Nevertheless, despite a lively debate concerning the validity of the underlying assumptions of the theory, its descriptive accuracy and its predictive ability, the model remains the backbone of population geography and as yet has not been superceded.

ASSIGNMENTS

1. (a) Describe the population pyramids shown in Figure 2.3, highlighting the
       main differences between them.
   (b) Explain the shapes of the pyramids by using Figure 2.2.

Table 2.2   Crude Birth Rates (CBR), Gross National Product (GNP) per capita and industry as a percentage of Gross Domestic Product (GDP) in India and Singapore (Source: World Bank, 1989)

	India			Singapore		
	GNP per capita $	Industry as % of GDP	CBR	GNP per capita $	Industry as % of GDP	CBR
1967	90	20	43	660	27	27
1969	90	21	42	840	30	23
1971	100	22	40	1080	34	23
1973	120	20	39	1580	36	22
1975	160	23	38	2540	36	18
1977	160	24	36	2320	39	18
1979	190	26	35	3880	39	17
1981	270	27	35	5450	41	17
1983	280	27	34	6930	41	17
1985	290	29	33	7620	40	17
1987	300	30	32	7940	40	16

2. (a) *What are the basic assumptions of the Demographic Transition Model?*
   (b) *List factors other than those identified by Notestein, which can affect birth and death rates in the Third World.*
3. (a) *With reference to Figure 2.2 and Figure 2.5, describe the demographic pathway taken by India and Singapore.*
   (b) *Using the statistics given in Table 2.2, discuss the importance of economic growth and industrialisation to the patterns already identified.*
   (c) *Suggest factors other than 'economic development' which may help to explain the demographic transition in these two countries.*

B. The Epidemiological Transition

Epidemiology is concerned with the causes, consequences and distribution of disease and death in human populations. Patterns of health and disease are integral components of population change. There have been many studies of disease occurrences through time and comparisons of the epidemiology of countries at different stages of economic development. The results of these studies have led many demographers to conclude that an epidemiological transition has paralleled the demographic transition. The theory suggests that as economic development takes place, pandemics (widespread epidemics) of infectious diseases associated with malnutrition and poverty such as tuberculosis and diarrhoea will be replaced by degenerative diseases of affluence, namely cancer and heart disease.

The main elements of the epidemiological transition are shown in Table 2.3. where four phases have been identified. Stage one is a period when the leading causes of death are tuberculosis, diarrhoea, malnutrition, parasitic and deficiency diseases, to which young women and children are particularly vulnerable. This phase is followed by two stages during which mortality begins to decline and economic prosperity increases. It is a period where although infection remains the leading cause of death, non-infectious diseases such as cancer and heart disease become more significant. The mortality decline during this period favours women and children, with infant and maternal mortality decreasing. The fourth phase is a period where mortality rates are low, and correspondingly the population comprises a large proportion of elderly people. As a result the prime killers are not the infectious diseases highlighted in the previous stages, but cancer, strokes and heart disease, with lung and viral infections remaining problems. By this stage the risks to females of all ages has decreased to such a level that, on average, life expectancy for women is a few years greater than for men. It is possible to hypothesise a fifth stage in this model, a period characterised by an increase in diseases associated with environmental pollution. This is a stage where economic progress has resulted in severe environmental problems, such as ozone depletion and high pollution levels. The impact on human populations might be to increase the incidence of deaths associated with environmental pollution, such as cancers, respiratory disease, brain damage and digestive disorders. At this stage all members of the community are at risk, children being the most vulnerable.

Table 2.3   The Epidemiological Transition (Source: adapted from Omran, 1971)

	Mortality level	Principal causes of death and disease	Groups most at risk
Stage 1	High.	Tuberculosis, diarrhoea, malnutrition, parasitic and deficiency diseases.	Young women and children.
Stage 2	A slight decline.	Endemic, parasitic and deficiency diseases. Industrial diseases begin to increase.	Young women and children.
Stage 3	A significant decline.	Infection remains the leading cause of death, but non-infectious diseases begin to be more significant.	Mortality decline favours women and children.
Stage 4	Low.	Heart disease, cancers and strokes are the major causes of death. Lung infections and viral diseases remain problems.	The risk to females of all ages declines.
Stage 5	Slight increase.	Main killers are the diseases of old age and affluence, with diseases associated with environmental pollution and viral infections growing in significance.	All members of population are at risk, especially children.

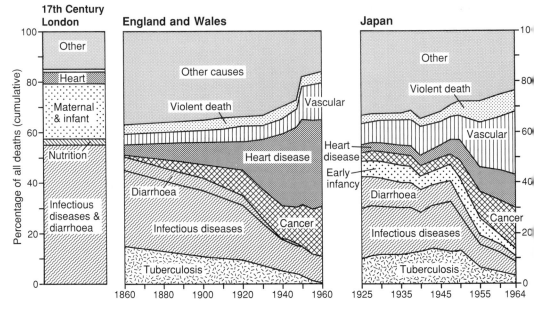

Figure 2.7   Chronological trends in the cause of death for both sexes in England and Wales, and Japan (Source: Omran, 1971)

A compilation of various studies of disease and death in England and Wales illustrated in Figure 2.7 demonstrates the epidemiological transition. It has been estimated that 75% of all deaths in seventeenth-century London could be attributed to infectious diseases, malnutrition and complications in childbirth, with cancer and heart disease accounting for less than 6% of the total. As Figure 2.7 shows, the decline in infectious disease in the UK is marked after the First World War, and the increase in deaths associated with heart disease is particularly striking after 1945. This transition is not unique to the UK; other developed nations such as USA and Japan can trace a similar trend. The determinants of such a transition from infectious to degenerative disease is complex and will be explored in Chapter 3.

ASSIGNMENTS

1. (a) Using Figure 2.2 and Table 2.3, describe the impact of the epidemiological transition on death rates.
   (b) What role does economic development play?
   (c) Which groups within the population are most vulnerable, and benefit most from such a transition?
2. (a) Describe the changes in the cause of death in Japan between 1925 and 1964, as shown in Figure 2.7.
   (b) How does this example reflect the epidemiological transition?

C. Zelinsky's Mobility Transition

The population of any area is not only the result of births and deaths, but can also be affected by in-migration and out-migration (see Chapter 1). The failure of the Demographic Transition Model to consider the impact of migration on population change is a serious omission. Any examination of population dynamics at a regional or national scale cannot ignore this very important demographic phenomenon. Recognising this deficiency in the theory, W. Zelinsky, in 1971, suggested a relationship not only between the demographic transition and economic development, but also mobility patterns. He stated that: *There are definite, patterned regularities in the growth of personal mobility through space-time during recent history, and these regularities comprise an essential component of the modernisation process.*

In other words, Zelinsky hypothesises that as economic development and hence the demographic transition progresses, a society changes from one where mobility is severely limited, to one where mobility is a necessary and desirable component of society. As this transition takes place, there will be inevitable changes in the function, frequency, duration, periodicity, distance and routing of movements. These changes in mobility patterns are the direct result of changing economic and social conditions, population pressure, the broadening of information fields (due to the communications revolution) and associated improvements in transport technology.

Zelinsky suggests that in stage one of the Demographic Transition Model, mobility is limited and dictated by local custom and movements associated with trade, religion and war. As the population moves into stages two and three of the model, increased population pressure results in two major types of mobility. First, movements of people to colonise new agricultural areas, as occurred from Europe to the USA in the last century, and secondly, a movement from the countryside to cities, as happened in the UK. These phases are characterised by agricultural and industrial innovations and are associated with massive urbanisation. By stage four, rural-to-urban mobility has slowed, but mobility between cities, or inter-urban mobility, has become significant as people move between urban areas in search of employment and opportunities. International mobility is also important at this stage, and movements of labour, as occurred from the Commonwealth to the UK in 1950s, is officially encouraged. The other important type of international mobility to surface at this stage is international tourism, fuelled by increased incomes and cheap and efficient methods of transportation. By stage five, nearly all movement is within or between cities, with a significant flow of people out of urban areas, looking for a better quality of life.

ASSIGNMENTS
1. *With reference to Figure 2.2 explain how migration may affect a country's demographic transition.*
2. *Zelinsky suggests that modernisation can alter mobility patterns. Using examples, examine why this may be the case.*

D. Case Studies

1. A declining and ageing population in Europe

Declining birth rates combined with increasing death rates have resulted in a number of countries entering stage five of the demographic transition model, and they are now experiencing declining population numbers. Germany, Denmark and Hungary are currently suffering population decline and it is predicted that by 2025 the populations of Belgium, Sweden, Italy, UK and Japan will also be decreasing. The region most severely affected is Western Europe, particularly the countries comprising the European Community (EC). In 1988 the population of the EC was 324.5 million; by 2040 it is expected to have fallen by 30 million to 290 million. The former territory of West Germany was one of the first countries to experience a population decline. Birth rates have been below the replacement level of 2.1 births per woman since 1969. The Population Reference Bureau has projected that if low birth rates persist then the population of the former territory of West Germany will drop to only 9.7 million in 2130 (in comparison with 61 million in 1987). Even if the fertility of former West Germany increases to replacement level, the Bureau projects that its population will continue to decline, stabilising at approximately 41 million.

West Germany, like other European countries, was aware of and concerned about the implications of very low fertility, in particular the ageing of the population. An ageing population is one where a large and growing proportion of that population is above retirement age. It is particularly associated with stages four and five of the demographic transition model.

In 1950, 8.5% of the world's population was over 60 years old, by 2025 it is estimated that this figure will have risen to 13.7%. The figure does however, hide large regional variations. By 2025 it is estimated that almost 25% of Europe's population will be over 60 years old, with over 22% of the US population in the same category (see Figure 2.8). The lowest proportion of elderly people will be found in Africa where the proportion will be less than 7%. On average the proportion of elderly people in the developed countries (24%) will be double that of the less developed countries (12%). In common with the rest of Europe the proportion of retired people living in England and Wales has increased from 4.7% in 1900 to 15.1% in 1988 and as Figure 2.9 shows is set to reach 19% by 2021.

The growing proportion of elderly people within a population present governments with serious economic problems, especially in the provision of state retirement pensions and health-care facilities. An increase in taxation on working adults to cover this extra spending seems inevitable. In 1987 expenditure by the British government on pensions was £300 million, and this is expected to rise to over £4000 million by the turn of the century. The Bank of Italy estimates that in 2010, social security payments will need to be set at 57% of earnings in order to care for the Italian elderly. In the former territory of West Germany the average annual pension costs for working age adults are expected to quadruple by 2030. Thus the

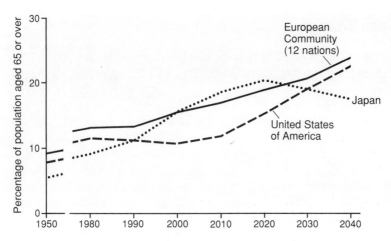

Figure 2.8   Trends in the proportions of people over 65 years old in the European Community, Japan and USA, 1950–2040 (Source: Evans, 1989)

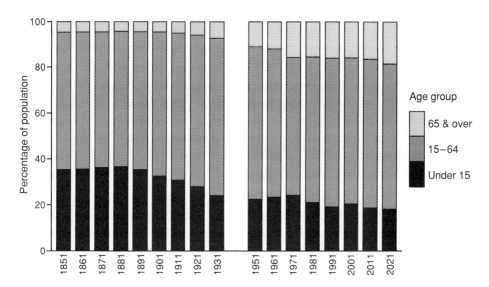

Figure 2.9   Age structure of the population of England and Wales, 1851–2021 (Source: Joshi, 1989)

increasing numbers of elderly people will place a heavy burden on the diminishing group of economically active adults within the population.

As a population ages the political power of the elderly in democratic societies seems set to rise. As the number of elderly people in the European population increases, they will inevitably come to form a greater and greater proportion of the electorate. Governments will have to take into account the needs and demands of

Plate 2.1   By the year 2025 it is estimated that 25% of Europe's population will be over 60 years old. This will place great social and economic pressures on society. These older folk take time off from shopping to relax in the sunshine. (Photograph: H.R. Barrett)

Plate 2.2   As the British population ages, the development of nursing homes and sheltered housing has become a booming business. This complex, similar to those being constructed all over the country, is located on Humberside. (Photograph: H.R. Barrett)

the elderly in order to secure their votes. This may result in political rivalry developing between those who are economically active and thus supporting the elderly, and the retired who wish to maintain and improve their standard of living. Governments may have to take very difficult decisions to appease the situation.

A solution to these economic and political problems for the nations of the EC could well be in-migration. In the next twenty years, 99.5% of all births will occur in the Third World, which will create a surplus of labour in these countries. This is a pool of unemployed labour which could be utilised in Europe. In-migration from the Third World could bring a number of benefits to the receiving countries. Not only would it provide labour to care for the elderly, but would also help to stabilise rising wages by supplementing the labour force and at the same time increase consumer demand. Thus in-migration would encourage economic growth within the EC. However, in-migration may prove to be unpopular with trades unions and may even fuel racial tensions. Nevertheless, it is clear that without in-migration European populations will continue to decline and age. The consequence of an ageing European population will inevitably be to present governments with serious economic and political problems, some of which are already becoming apparent.

2. The limited transition of the Islamic countries

There are 40 countries in the world where believers in the Islamic faith, known as Muslims, are in a majority. In addition there are seven countries where Muslims comprise 25-49% of the population. These 47 countries form the core of the Islamic world. There are, however, nine other countries with sizeable Islamic minorities, including China, India and USSR. It was estimated that there were 980 million Muslims worldwide in 1988, accounting for 20% of the world's population. By the year 2020 it is estimated that the number of Muslims will have doubled, accounting for 23% of the world's population.

Although Islam originated in present-day Saudi Arabia with the birth of the prophet Mohammed in the late sixth century AD, it has spread well beyond the Arab world. Figure 2.10 shows the current extent of the Islamic socio-cultural milieu. The Islamic culture is found as far west as Senegal in West Africa, eastwards to Indonesia, and has spread north into Europe, notably Albania. Geographically the largest number of Islamic states is in the Middle East, a region that includes North Africa and West Asia. However, the most populous Islamic nation is Indonesia, with over 156 million adherents of the faith. Pakistan has the second largest Muslim population of over 104 million, followed by Bangladesh with 93 million Muslims.

The most remarkable aspect of Islamic countries is their universally high crude birth and death rates. The demographic characteristics of Islamic nations as compared to the other main groupings of countries is shown in Table 2.4. This table shows that the average crude birth rate of the Islamic group of countries is 42.1, which is 25% higher than other developing countries. Correspondingly the average crude death rate in the Islamic countries was 13.8, which is 37% higher than the other developing countries. These figures indicate a group of countries farther behind in the demographic transition than other categories of nations.

The position within the demographic transition of those Islamic countries with a population of over five million is shown in Figure 2.11. From this graph it can be seen that many Islamic countries are still in stages one and two of the transition, with a few countries entering stage three. The diagram illustrates also that there are large disparities between Islamic countries. Crude death rates vary from 6 per 1000 in Malaysia to 23 in Guinea Conakry, with Kuwait, not included on the diagram, experiencing the lowest crude death rate of only 3 per 1000. Crude birth rates, however, show the greatest disparity, with Indonesia recording a birth rate of 29 per 1000 and Côte d'Ivoire, Niger and Mali all recording a staggering 51. The

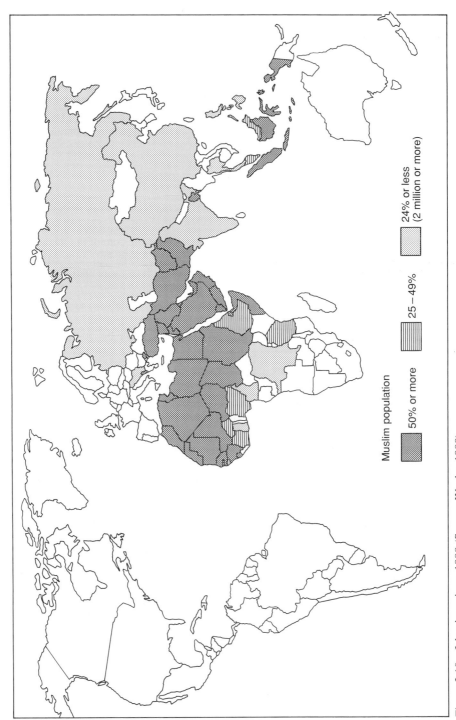

Figure 2.10   Islamic nations, 1988 (Source: Weeks, 1988)

Muslim population

50% or more

25 – 49%

24% or less
(2 million or more)

Table 2.4   Demographic characteristics of Islamic nations compared with other categories
of nations, 1988 (Source: Weeks, 1988)

	Islamic Nations	Other Developing Nations	Centrally Planned Economies	Developed Nations
Number of nations	47	94	7	25
Average crude birth rate per 1000 population	42.1	33.6	15.0	13.1
Average crude death rate per 1000 population	13.8	10.1	11.6	9.4
Average rate of natural increase (%)	2.8	2.3	0.4	0.3
Average % of population under 15 years old	43	39	23	20

United Arab Emirates, not included on the graph, records the lowest crude birth
rate of this group of countries, of 23 per 1000.

The Islamic culture zone includes some of the poorest countries in the world,
such as Ethiopia and Bangladesh, as well as some of the most economically
advantaged countries in the world, the high-income oil exporting countries. These
countries, which include Saudi Arabia, Kuwait, United Arab Emirates, Brunei,

Figure 2.11   The position of Islamic countries (with a population of over 5 million)
within the Demographic Transition, 1987 (Source: World Development Report, 1989)

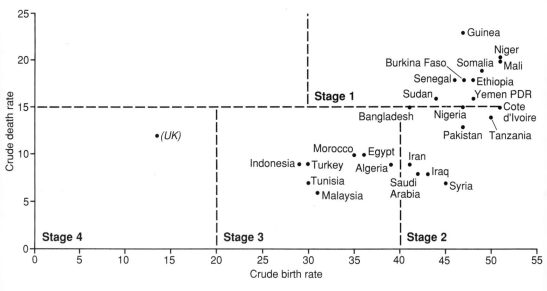

Qatar and Oman, all have income levels similar to Western Europe and according to the Demographic Transition Model would be expected to have similar demographic characteristics. However, although these countries experience death rates comparable to Western Europe, as Table 2.1 shows they have very much higher fertility levels, with Oman and Saudi Arabia recording crude birth rates of over 40 per 1000. Despite having similar and in some cases higher income levels than Western Europe, the high-income oil exporting countries are at an earlier stage in the demographic transition. This demonstrates that economic development is not the only factor determining the demographic transition.

Population geographers are curious to know why the demographic characteristics of Islamic countries are different from countries with similar income levels. Although Islam is not regarded as an exclusive influence, demographers believe that it does contribute by creating a distinctive demographic environment.

Contrary to popular belief, Islam is not against contraception, and abortion is legal in most countries. However, governments play a varied role. A number of governments encourage fertility, including Libya, Iraq, Kuwait, Oman, Qatar, Saudi Arabia and United Arab Emirates. These are all oil-rich Arab countries and apart from Iraq and Saudi Arabia have populations of less than five million. Other governments are worried about high birth rates and have implemented population planning policies, notably Egypt, Bangladesh, Indonesia, Pakistan, Morocco and Tunisia. These are all countries experiencing population pressure and environmental degradation. The fact that many of these countries still have high birth rates, despite a commitment to reduce fertility, suggests that other factors must be considered. Of special interest are those aspects of Islam that govern marriage and family life, including social relationships between men and women.

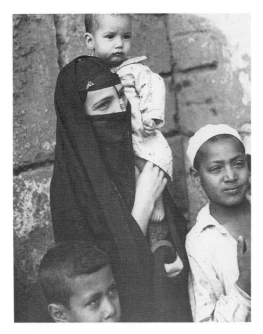

Plate 2.3   Women in many Islamic countries wear a veil in public, as does this Egyptian woman pictured with her children. This is in response to the command in the Koran that women should cover themselves.
(Photograph: J. Allan Cash Ltd)

Islam strongly promotes marriage, and divorce is considered very undesirable. The religion supports the dominance of males in society and is patriarchal. Under Islamic law men may have as many as four wives at one time, providing they can support them. The eldest male has full authority over the family. This often leads to arranged, early marriages of daughters and the seclusion of women in the home. The result is often a society where women's status is inferior to that of men, and is indicative of a socio-economic environment where high fertility prevails.

The status of women within a community is difficult to measure, first because it varies from country to country and secondly because data is not always available. It is generally accepted that the status of women depends on their degree of access to and control over material and social resources within the family, community and society in general. This includes access to education, healthcare facilities, access and control of land, labour force participation as well as political emancipation. Two measures of female status are compared for three groups of countries in Figure 2.12. This shows that women in Islamic societies are more likely to be married by the age of nineteen and least likely to have a secondary education than women in other parts of the world. Female labour participation rates are also low in Islamic countries, with an average of only 13% of women working as compared to 60% in UK. This suggests that Islamic women enjoy a lower status within society than other groups of women.

The Islamic world is demographically distinctive, characterised by high birth and death rates, and as a result tends to be farther behind in the demographic transition than other categories of nations with similar income levels. This suggests that factors other than economic development are responsible. The inferior status of women within Islamic society is one important consideration. Global data shows that low female status is positively correlated with high fertility, regardless of government population planning policies. As this case study shows, the improved status of women is not necessarily dependent on economic development, but is principally culturally determined. The Demographic Transition Model is therefore seriously flawed by neglecting to include social factors, and as such might not be applicable to the demographic experiences of countries with different cultural backgrounds.

Figure 2.12   Status of women in three groups of countries (Source: Weeks, 1988)

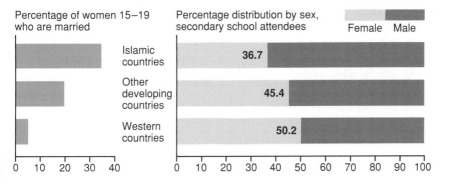

ASSIGNMENTS

1. (a) *By examining the population pyramid on Figure 2.3, explain why the population of former West Germany is predicted to decline if birth rates continue at current levels.*
   (b) *Sketch what the population pyramid of former West Germany would look like under current birth and death rates in the year 2010.*
   (c) *Describe the hypothetical age composition of the former West German population in 2010.*
2. (a) *What is meant by an ageing population?*
   (b) *Using Figure 2.8 describe the trends of ageing populations in EC, Japan and USA.*
   (c) *What are the implications for countries experiencing this phenomenon?*
3. (a) *Using Figure 2.11, Figure 2.6 and Table 2.4, comment on the demographic situation of Islamic countries as compared with non-Islamic countries.*
   (b) *With reference to Section A, discuss the validity of the assumptions of the Demographic Transition Model in explaining the population experience of Islamic countries.*

Key Ideas

Introduction

1. Although the number of people being born continues to increase, the world's population growth is slowing and is estimated to stabilise at 10.2 billion by the end of the next century.
2. The present-day global population is the result of two population surges. The first was a surge in European populations beginning in the eighteenth century and lasting approximately 200 years. The second is the surge that has occurred in the Third World since the Second World War.

A. The Demographic Transition

1. The demographic transition suggests a relationship between population change and socio-economic development. The result is a five-stage model demonstrating the relationship between birth and death rates as modernisation takes place.
2. As a population progresses through the demographic transition, the age and sex structure of the population will change from one that is dominated by young people to a population with a large proportion of elderly people.
3. The demographic transition has been used as a descriptive model and as such fits a number of cases.
4. The Demographic Transition Model is also used to predict the development of populations. However, problems arise when using the model to predict Third World population evolution. These anomalies have led many geographers to question the validity of the model.

70

B. The Epidemiological Transition

Demographers suggest that an epidemiological transition has paralleled the demographic transition, with disease patterns changing as economic development progresses.

C. Zelinsky's Mobility Transition

1. The demographic transition omits to consider migration, an important component of population change.
2. Zelinsky suggests that mobility patterns change as economic development occurs, and that each stage of the demographic transition is characterised by different forms and intensity of mobility.

D. Case Studies

1. The later stages of the demographic transition are characterised by low birth rates and are associated with a growing proportion of elderly people within the population.
2. Ageing populations present governments in the developed world with serious economic and political problems.
3. Muslims comprise 20% of the world's population and form a demographically distinct grouping, with higher than expected birth and death rates.
4. Although Islam is not regarded as the only influence, it contributes to high fertility levels indirectly through its attitude towards women.
5. This case study demonstrates that cultural factors are as important as economic factors in determining population structure.

Additional Activities

1. (a) With reference to the Demographic Transition Model, describe the demographic trends shown in Figure 2.13 (see page 72).
   (b) For the years 1960, 1990 and 2010, calculate the dependency ratio (see below) for the seven global regions shown in Figure 2.13.
   (c) Discuss your results, highlighting the implications of ageing populations to the future economic development of these regions.
2. (a) With reference to some of the examples given in this chapter and Chapter 1, discuss the validity of the assumptions of the Demographic Transition Model. Note especially the cultural and environmental considerations.

Dependency Ratio
This statistic expresses the ratio of unproductive and hence dependent members of a population, i.e. the young (less than 15 years) and elderly (over 60/65 years), to the population of working age (15-60/65 years).

The Ratio is calculated as follows:

$$\frac{\text{Population less than 15 years} + \text{Population over 60/65 years}}{\text{Population between 15 and 60/65 years}} \times 100$$

The result shows how many dependants each working person is indirectly supporting. The statistic allows for valid comparisons between regions as well as through time. The Ratio can be adjusted to show a ratio of young or elderly people to the working population. These would then be termed the Young Dependency Ratio or Ageing Dependency Ratio. In conjunction with the Dependency Ratio these are useful in determining the weighting of the young and the elderly in the community.

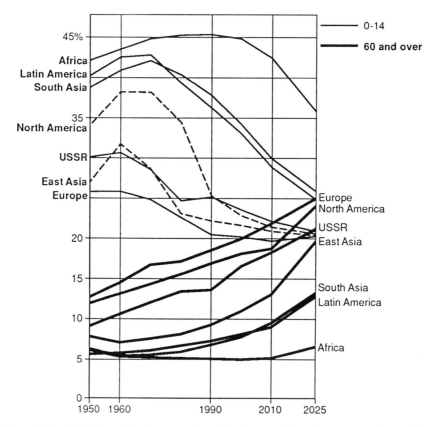

Figure 2.13   Global trends in the proportion of 0–14 year-olds and persons aged over 60 in the population, 1950 to 2025 (Source: United Nations, *World Population at the turn of the century*, Population Studies series 111, 1989)

Mortality as a Component of Population Change

Introduction

This chapter examines mortality as a component of population change. Unlike fertility control, mortality control is a less controversial topic in most societies and the adoption of death control measures has been significant. The result has been a general lowering of death rates. This decline in mortality rates began in Sweden in the eighteenth century and Britain in the nineteenth century and spread to the rest of Europe and the developed world. The present century has seen the decline of death rates in the poorer countries of the world, most notably Latin America and Asia. This reduction in mortality levels has serious implications for population growth, size and age structure. Mortality control means that people live longer. Longevity combined with reduced birth rates produces an ageing population (see Chapter 2). It has been estimated that by the year 2025 almost 14% of the world's population will be over 60 years old, as compared with only 9% in 1975.

Mortality can be measured in a number of ways.

(a) The simplest is the *crude death rate* (CDR) which is the number of deaths in a specific period per 1000 of the population. This measure is, however, distorted by age structure variations and explains why some Third World countries have a much lower CDR than advanced nations. Table 3.1 demonstrates that Kuwait, Saudi Arabia, Singapore, Mexico, Brazil, Jamaica and Sri Lanka all have much lower CDRs than UK. This can be explained by the much younger age structure of these countries. Because the population comprises a large proportion of young people, fewer people per 1000 will die, but the CDR may increase dramatically as those young people move into middle age.

(b) In order that mortality statistics may be more fairly compared, *age-specific mortality rates* may be used. These express the number of deaths of persons of a certain age per 1000 of the population in that age group. It is conventional to use five- or ten-year groupings. Because of the importance of infant deaths as indicators of social and environmental conditions, these are often examined separately. The *infant mortality rate* (IMR) is the number of deaths of infants under one year old per 1000 live births in a given year. The IMRs of a selection of countries are given in Table 3.1, indicating the vast range in IMRs between countries at different levels of economic development.

(c) The comparison of two or more countries using age-specific data is difficult and often a summary measure is more useful. The one often used is the *standardised*

Table 3.1 Mortality indices for a selection of countries at various stages of development (Source: World Bank, 1988)

	GNP per capita $ (1986)	CDR 1985	IMR 1985	Life expectancy 1986
USA	17 480	9	10	75
Sweden	13 160	11	6	77
UK	8 870	12	9	75
Kuwait	13 890	3	19	73
Saudi Arabia	6 950	8	64	63
Singapore	7 410	5	9	73
Mexico	1 850	6	48	68
Brazil	1 810	8	65	65
Jamaica	840	6	19	73
Nigeria	640	16	104	51
Sri Lanka	400	6	29	70
Kenya	300	12	74	57
India	290	12	86	57
Uganda	230	18	105	48
Ethiopia	120	19	155	46

death rate (SDR). This is a figure that indicates what the CDR would be if the population being studied had the same age and sex composition as a population that is being used as the standard. This standard may be a different country or even historical data of the same country, to enable comparisons to be made. The SDR has little intrinsic meaning. It is only meaningful in relation to other SDRs based on the same standard and the standard itself and is therefore only used in comparative studies.

(d) Of more use, in terms of comparability, is the index, *life expectancy at birth*. It is the average number of years that would be lived by a group of people born in the same year, assuming that age-specific death rates of that year are maintained throughout the life history of the group. It is an index that is difficult to calculate as it is normally derived from national life tables. Nevertheless it is a useful comparative index, often giving a more accurate insight into mortality conditions within a country than CDR. For example, on Table 3.1 of all those countries recording CDRs lower than the UK, none had a higher life expectancy at birth. By looking at the table it becomes clear that life expectancy figures are highly correlated to IMR, which is not surprising as the IMR is taken into account in the calculation of the life expectancy figures. Life expectancy figures are therefore a fairly meaningful and easily comparable index of mortality levels within a country.

A. Geography of Mortality

The United Nations' estimate of the average crude death rate of the world's population in 1985 was 11 per 1000. This figure disguises large spatial variations,

Table 3.2 Crude Death Rates and Infant Mortality Rates for the major regions of the world
(Source: UN Demographic Yearbook, 1988; UN Population Bulletin, 1982)

	CDR (1985)	IMR (1980)
Africa		
West	18	146
East	18	127
North	12	117
Central	18	128
South	14	103
America		
North	9	14
South	8	79
Central	8	65
Caribbean	8	65
Asia		
China	7	49
Japan	7	9
Other East Asia	6	36
South	13	131
South-East	11	120
Western	10	110
Europe		
West	11	13
South	10	23
East	11	23
North	12	12
Oceania		
Australia & New Zealand	8	13
Other Oceania	10	73
USSR	9	29
World Total	11	89

as shown in Table 3.2. Central Africa has the highest CDR of 18 per 1000, together with East and West Africa. CDRs in all parts of Africa exceed the global average. Southern Asia and Northern Europe also exceed the average to a lesser extent. Within these areas there are exceptions: in Africa, Egypt (9), Mauritius (7) and Tunisia (10) have lower than average CDRs, as do Pakistan (10), Sri Lanka (6) and Thailand (8) in Asia. In Europe, Holland (9), Finland (10) and Spain (8) stand out as below the world average. The lowest estimated CDRs (below 5) are recorded for the Cook Islands, Costa Rica and United Arab Emirates. The lowest CDR of three per 1000 was recorded in Kuwait.

Many of the countries in these regions owe their high mortality to very high IMRs. In 1980 the United Nations estimated the world average IMR to be 89 per

1000 live births. All the regions experiencing above average CDRs also recorded IMRs above 100 per 1000, with West Africa reaching a staggering 146 per 1000. Once again, these figures disguise large spatial variations. The countries experiencing the highest IMRs are Afghanistan (181), Sierra Leone (179) and The Gambia (174). Those countries experiencing the lowest IMRs of six or less are Japan, Iceland, Finland and Sweden. The United Nations World Health Organisation (WHO) has called for a reduction in IMRs to 50 or less per 1000 by the end of the century. This is a target that many countries will find difficult to achieve.

High CDRs and high IMRs result in low expectation of life at birth. Figure 3.1 shows the world pattern of life expectancy by country. The countries recording the lowest life expectancy at birth are Guinea Bissau (39 years), Sierra Leone (41), The Gambia (43) and Niger (44). All these countries are in West Africa and are some of the poorest countries in the world. The highest life expectancy at birth of 78 years is recorded by Japan and Australia, followed by Holland, France, Sweden, Norway and Switzerland, all scoring 77 years. These are some of the richest nations in the world and with the exception of Australia and Japan are all in Western Europe. This has led some specialists to correlate mortality, especially infant mortality, with economic development.

World variations in mortality are smaller than variations in fertility with CDRs evening out between 10 and 13 per 1000, depending on the age structure of the population. However, as is shown in Figure 3.2, there is a clear pattern of low CDRs in Europe, Oceania and the Americas, increasing in southern Asia and reaching a peak in central Africa. Infant mortality rates and life expectancy patterns, shown in Figures 3.1 and 3.3, follow the same pattern.

ASSIGNMENTS

1. (a) Using Table 3.2 and Figure 3.2 describe the global pattern of Crude Death Rates.
   (b) How would the use of Standardised Death Rates alter the patterns you have described?
2. (a) Examine Figure 3.3 and describe the pattern shown.
   (b) What relationship is suggested between Infant Mortality Rates and the annual number of births?

B. Causes of Mortality

There are marked differences in the causes of mortality between the developed and the developing countries. The developed world, with an older population structure, reveals a pattern of degenerative diseases. As shown in Figure 3.4, heart disease, strokes and other circulatory diseases contribute 48% of deaths, with cancers contributing a further 19%. The developing countries have a more youthful population structure and a mortality pattern which is dominated by child deaths. For this reason the causes of death are associated with diseases of youth. Figure 3.4 shows that parasitic and infective disorders including gastro-enteritis and tuberculosis are important, contributing over 40% of deaths. The cause of death can be attributed

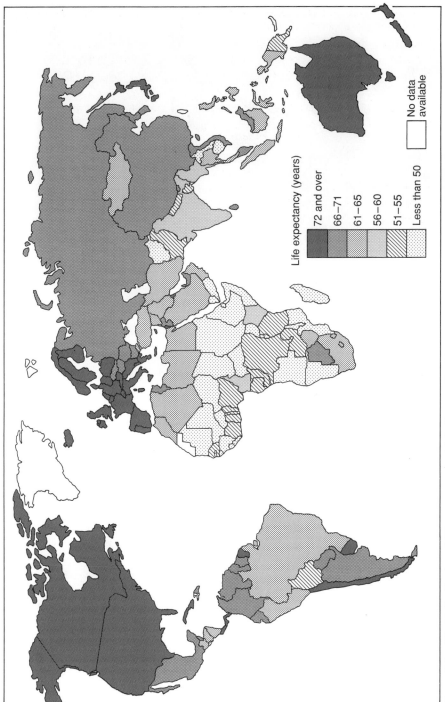

Figure 3.1   World distribution of life expectancy at birth (Source: World Bank, 1990, UN Demographic Yearbook, 1986)

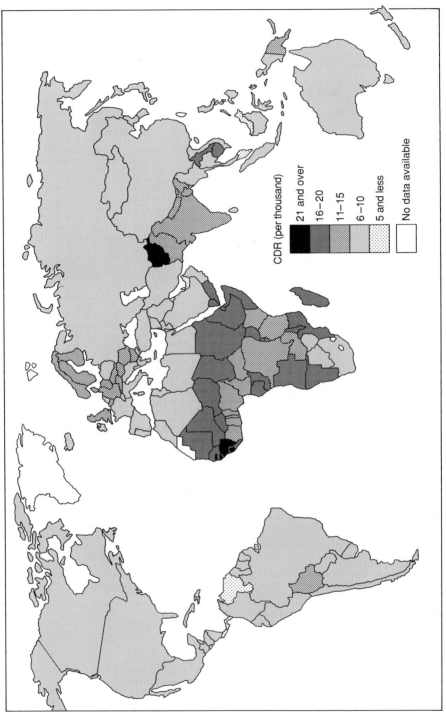

Figure 3.2   World distribution of crude death rates (Source: World Bank, 1990, UN Demographic Yearbook, 1986)

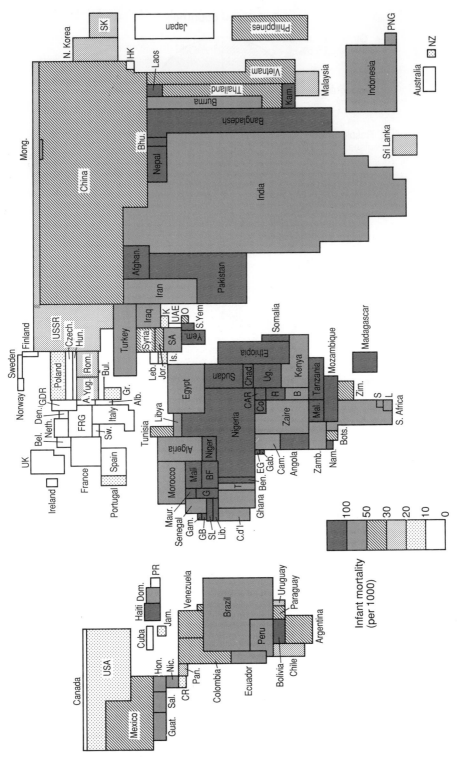

Figure 3.3 World distribution of estimated infant mortality rates (Sizes of countries are proportional to the estimated average annual number of births, 1988 (Source: World Bank, 1990, UN Demographic Yearbook, 1986/UN Population Bulletin, 1982)

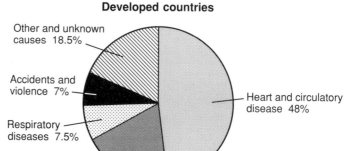

Developed countries

Other and unknown causes 18.5%

Accidents and violence 7%

Respiratory diseases 7.5%

Cancers 19%

Heart and circulatory disease 48%

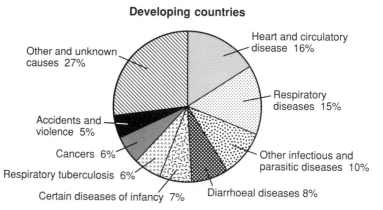

Developing countries

Other and unknown causes 27%

Accidents and violence 5%

Cancers 6%

Respiratory tuberculosis 6%

Certain diseases of infancy 7%

Heart and circulatory disease 16%

Respiratory diseases 15%

Other infectious and parasitic diseases 10%

Diarrhoeal diseases 8%

Figure 3.4   Major causes of death in developed and developing countries in the 1980s (Source: World Health Organisation (WHO))

to two major variables, *environmental factors* and *socio-economic factors*, or a combination of both.

1. Environmental factors

Environmental factors can have a dramatic and unpredictable affect on mortality levels. Droughts and floods have a clear and obvious affect on death rates in the areas experiencing them. Other, less dramatic environmental conditions, such as a hot-humid climate, may have a less obvious impact, but nevertheless can influence mortality by stimulating conditions favourable to certain diseases and pests. Air pollution, for example, has been associated with the incidence of certain cancers and respiratory diseases. Exposure to ultra-violet rays has been shown to have a positive relationship with skin cancer, and higher than average mortality rates are reported during periods of extreme temperatures. Although environmental factors are important in determining death rates they are not easy to quantify, isolate or even identify, as many environmental factors are related to and affected by socio-economic changes.

2. Socio-economic factors

Socio-economic factors which have an impact on mortality levels include housing conditions: mortality rates are higher in damp, over-crowded dwellings. Sanitation and availability of pure water have a direct impact on mortality, as does nutritional status and accessibility of health care facilities. The social class of an individual can also affect life expectancy. A number of studies have demonstrated that life expectancy is higher for professional people than for unskilled workers in both developed and less developed countries. Although it is recognised that socio-economic factors contribute greatly to mortality levels, it is extremely difficult to measure precisely the impact each has on the death rate, because most factors are interrelated and do not act in isolation. Improvements in socio-economic conditions, however, have a demonstrable impact on mortality decline. Some scholars suggest that socio-economic factors are more important than environmental factors in affecting mortality decline. This is because many environmental factors can be tempered, and some of their consequences controlled, by socio-economic advances. This leads to the conclusion that the impact of environmental factors on mortality decreases as socio-economic advances take place within a society.

Plate 3.1   Back to back houses were commonplace in most cities in nineteenth-century Britain. This picture taken in Staithes, Yorkshire, in the last century, demonstrates the crowded living conditions of most urban families. In these potentially unsanitary conditions it is no surprise that mortality rates were high. (Photograph: Mary Evans Picture Library)

Monitor a 'quality' newspaper for a given period (2-4 weeks).

(a) Note any environmental incidents that have resulted in loss of life.

(b) Classify the incidents (i.e. earthquakes, floods, etc.) and plot them on a map.

(c) Use proportional circles to illustrate the number of deaths associated with each incident.

(d) Discuss your results, highlighting the role socio-economic factors could play in preventing future loss of life in such incidents.

C. Causes of Mortality Decline

It is usually assumed that as a society develops, its mortality rates will decline (see Chapter 2). This happened in Europe in the eighteenth and nineteenth centuries and is happening at present in the Third World. Mortality decline is a complex issue, attributed to the interplay of four factors which are shown in Figure 3.5: sanitary reforms; changing disease patterns; advances in medical care; and improvements in living standards.

1. Sanitary reforms

Sanitary reforms aim to eliminate those environmental conditions favourable to the spread of disease. They are effective only if they succeed in reducing human contact with infectious micro-organisms. Accurate knowledge of those environmental conditions which spread infection is vital. There are five routes by which human beings can be infected with disease: water; food; vectors, or carriers; air; and personal contact. Examples of disease types, how they are spread and by what method they can be controlled, is shown in Table 3.3.

The spread of certain infections can be controlled according to their transmission route. The infectious diseases most readily controlled are those which are spread

Figure 3.5   A simple model of factors affecting mortality levels (Source: adapted from Woods, 1984)

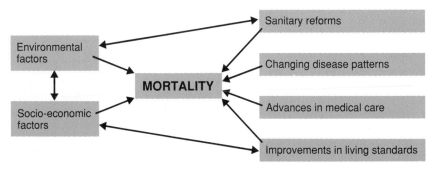

Table 3.3   Categories of diseases, mechanisms of spread and methods of control

Disease type	Example disease	Mechanism of spread	Method of control
Water-borne	Cholera Typhoid	Water contaminated by urine or excrement	Purification of water Efficient sewage disposal
Food-borne	Dysentery Para-typhoid Gastro-enteritis	Contaminated food or water, especially milk	Food hygiene Pasteurisation of milk Health education
Vector-borne	Rabies Bubonic plague Malaria Typhus fever	A complex relationship between the micro-organism, the vector or carrier of the micro-organism and the human host. Insects often act as vectors	Removing vector usually by destroying its habitat or breeding ground, i.e. clearing bush and draining swamps, etc.
Air-borne	Bronchitis Pneumonia Respiratory tuberculosis Scarlet fever	Spread either directly by tiny water droplets or indirectly by dust from bedding, clothes, carpets, etc.	Isolating infected individual Increasing ventilation Reducing over-crowding
Personal contact	Sexually transmitted diseases Scabies Trachoma	By direct personal contact	Health education

Plate 3.2 Open drains like this one in Banjul, the capital of The Gambia, are insanitary and provide the ideal environment for the breeding of mosquitoes, the vector agent for malaria, which is endemic in this part of the world. (Photograph: H.R. Barrett)

by water. This requires the purification of water supplies and the installation of efficient sewage disposal. In the economically advanced countries of the West it is relatively easy to control water-borne diseases, but more difficult to control diseases spread by food, personal contact and vectors. It is virtually impossible to control air-borne infections. In the Third World the provision of safe water and efficient sewage disposal is constrained by limited resources. At the end of 1983, WHO found that about 75% of people living in urban areas in the developing world had access to piped water, with 61% served through house connections. However, in rural areas only 40% of the population had access to safe water, and the coverage of sanitation services is less extensive. Just over 50% of urban dwellers have sewage disposal facilities, and only 36% have connections to public sewers. The Third World today has implemented few sanitary reforms. A recent estimate suggests that the minimum cost of providing safe water to all those who need it in the Third World would be approximately $300 billion, i.e. 15% of their gross national product (GNP). In the Third World, vector-borne diseases are more common than in temperate regions and there have been many programmes aimed at eradicating insect vectors. Their success has been debatable.

2. Changing disease patterns

It is widely suggested by population geographers that a change in the character of infectious diseases may account for mortality decline, independent of any medical advances or changes in socio-economic conditions. This is a complex issue, and is also the subject of much debate. There is evidence that the relationship between the human host and the micro-organisms of certain air-borne diseases has altered, but the evidence for change amongst other groups of diseases is negligible.

84

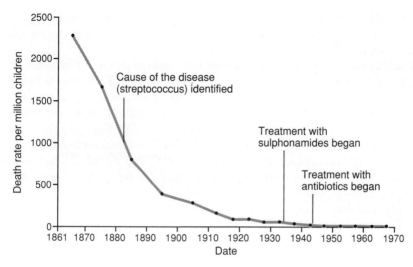

Figure 3.6   Trend in the death rate of children under 15 years in England and Wales from scarlet fever (Source: McKeown, 1976)

There is little doubt that the decline in mortality from scarlet fever, an air-borne disease, can be attributed to a change in the nature of the disease. Scarlet fever was first described in 1676 as a mild disease, since when it has exhibited at least four cycles of severity and remission. The disease was particularly virulent in the late eighteenth century and in the mid-nineteenth century, reaching a peak in 1863. Since then it has declined and is now a relatively minor illness. This is due to the unstable relationship between the host and the parasite. Death rates from scarlet fever of children under 15 years for the period 1861 to 1970 in England and Wales are shown in Figure 3.6. This graph shows a rapid decline in the fatality of the disease from 1861 until 1900, followed by a slower decline in this century. This decline took place despite the fact that there was no effective treatment of the disease until 1935.

It would appear that some air-borne diseases, particularly scarlet fever, have experienced some genetic change in their character in the last hundred years, resulting in fewer fatalities. However, in the other disease categories it is more difficult to relate declining mortality to changing disease patterns because of the complicated relationship between the environment and socio-economic improvements.

3. Improved medicine and health care

Until recently it was taken for granted that mortality decline in nineteenth-century Europe was the result of medical advances, including the expansion of hospitals, changes in health education and improvements in medicines and treatments. However, there is now a lively debate amongst population specialists as to the role of medicine in this decline. It is accepted that medical advances were important, but that they have been much more influential in the recent mortality decline in the Third World.

Many demographers now accept that the full impact of chemically mass-produced drugs, or *chemotherapy*, was not felt until after the Second World War. It therefore cannot explain or account for the decline in the death rate that occurred before that date. Tuberculosis, the largest single cause of death in England and Wales in the mid-nineteenth century, had been declining since 1830. Figure 3.7 shows quite clearly that this decline was occurring long before effective treatment for tuberculosis began with the introduction of antibiotics in 1947 and the BCG immunisation programme of the 1950s. Since these dates there has been a more rapid fall in mortality from the disease.

In contrast, the pattern of diphtheria deaths shown in Figure 3.8 does correlate with the treatment of the disease. Anti-toxins were first used in diphtheria cases in 1900, resulting in a decline in deaths from the disease. That decline has been followed by an even greater reduction in deaths since the national immunisation campaign began in 1941. The control of polio (poliomyelitis) by vaccination is also heralded as a triumph for modern science. Polio vaccine has been in common use in England and Wales since the 1950s.

With the exception of smallpox, chemotherapy and the development of vaccines did not have a significant effect on mortality from infectious diseases before the twentieth century. It was only after 1935 that chemotherapeutic agents such as sulphonamides and antibiotics became available. Effective treatment for typhoid and typhus was not available until the 1950s and penicillin was not widely in use until 1945.

Figure 3.7   Trend in the death rate in England and Wales from tuberculosis (Source: McKeown, 1976)

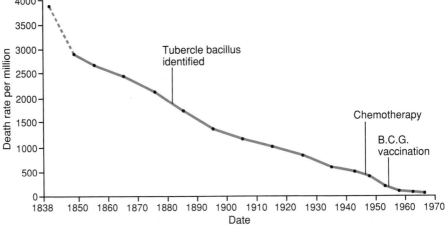

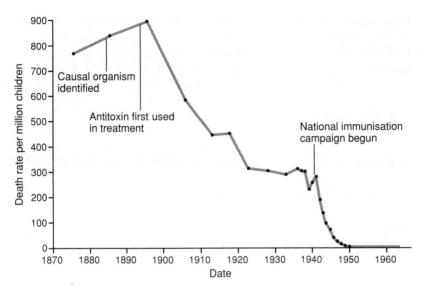

Figure 3.8   Trend in the death rate of children under 15 years in England and Wales from diphtheria (Source: McKeown, 1976)

4. Improvements in living standards

It has been demonstrated that the incidence of many air, water, food and vector-borne diseases will inevitably decline with rising living standards and improved nourishment. Nutritional status directly affects an individual's resistance to influenza, pneumonia, bronchitis, diarrhoea and tuberculosis, since protein malnourishment impairs the production of circulating anti-bodies. Rising living standards and better hygiene standards have meant that many insect vectors, such as fleas and lice, disappear. However, with over 75% of the world's population living in the Third World, most in extremely poor conditions, with over one billion people undernourished and between 13 and 18 million people dying from hunger a year, it has been suggested that the Third World needs an improved standard of living and food supply more than it needs Western medicine. Improvements in living standards, which are usually associated with improved nutritional status, can improve mortality rates and in conjunction with the other factors outlined above could have a significant effect in reducing death rates in the poorer countries of the world.

ASSIGNMENTS
Study Figure 3.4 and Table 3.3.
(a) Describe the major causes of death in the developing world.
(b) What would be the impact of introducing the control mechanisms described in Table 3.3 on the pattern described?

*(c) What impact would vaccination campaigns have on the principal causes of
death highlighted in Figure 3.4?*

*(d) Explain how improved living standards in the developing world can reduce
death rates.*

D. Case Studies

1. Mortality decline in nineteenth-century England and Wales

The standardised death rates for England and Wales for the period 1840-1970 are
shown in Figure 3.9. They demonstrate that although death rates have been falling,
mortality rates are consistently higher for males. There are also differences between
age groups, between urban and rural areas, within towns and between occupations.
The exact analysis of these variations is difficult because the civil registration of
births, deaths and marriages, known as *vital events*, did not begin in England and
Wales until 1837 and in Scotland until 1855. After these dates, age at death and
cause of death were recorded. However, in the nineteenth and early twentieth
centuries, when medical science was still in its infancy, identifying cause of death
was problematic and at times inaccurate.

Despite these problems it is clear that since the 1880s, England and Wales have
experienced a declining mortality rate, the result of which is that the life expectancy

Figure 3.9   Trend in the Standardised Death Rate in England and Wales (Source:
McKeown, 1976)

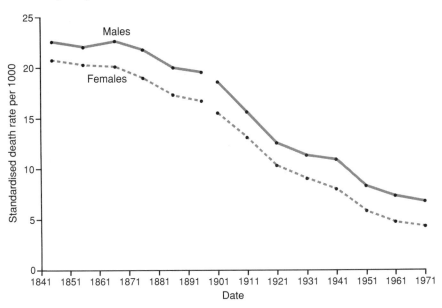

at birth of people living in this part of the UK has increased. In the nineteenth century, life expectation increased from 36 to 50 years and is currently at 76 years. In spite of the poor data base, it is possible to consider the causes of mortality in nineteenth century England and Wales and to examine the changes that occurred in order to assess the importance of the four factors discussed in Section C above.

Evaluating the importance of the four possible causes of mortality decline is not easy. Thomas McKeown has presented a model to explain the decline in mortality in the second half of the nineteenth century. The model is shown in Figure 3.10. Between 1848/1854 and 1901 mortality fell by 22% in England and Wales. By taking this 22%, which is the total decline during that period, as 100%, McKeown has calculated the proportions of the decline which are attributable to the major disease combinations. He calculates that 44% of the mortality decline was the result of a reduction in deaths attributable to air-borne diseases, 33% to a reduction in deaths associated with water- and food-borne diseases, 15% to other conditions associated with micro-organisms, and only 8% with conditions not associated with micro-organisms. Therefore over 75% of the mortality decline in the period can be attributed to a reduction in deaths from air, water and food-borne diseases. A closer look at the categories reveals that a reduction in respiratory tuberculosis is responsible for 34% of the decline, with scarlet fever and diptheria (12.5%) also significant in the air-borne disease category. It should be noted that there was an 10.5% *increase*

Figure 3.10   Cause-specific influences on mortality decline in England and Wales, 1848–54 to 1901, in percentages (Source: adapted from McKeown, 1976 and Woods, 1984)

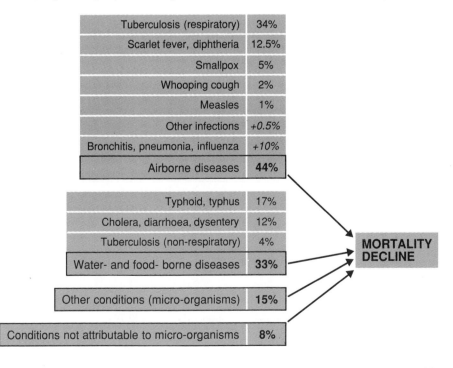

in deaths in this category associated with bronchitis, pneumonia, influenza, and other infections. This can be explained by increasing urbanisation and industrialisation, with associated air pollution and crowded living conditions. The decline in water- and food-borne diseases can be explained by the declining fatalities from cholera, diarrhoea, dysentry, typhoid and typhus.

It is necessary to ask why fatality from diseases such as respiratory tuberculosis, scarlet fever and cholera, typhus and typhoid decreased during this period. McKeown suggests that there are three reasons: increased standards of living and diet, sanitary reform measures and changes in disease character.

The demographic changes which occurred in nineteenth-century England and Wales must be understood in the context of the great social and economic changes which began in the mid-eighteenth century. The expansion in industry and the changes in agricultural methods and practice brought about a transformation in British society. Between the middle of the nineteenth century and the beginning of the twentieth century, Britain moved from a rural-based economy to the world's leading industrial and colonial power. Not surprisingly, the occupation structure of the population changed profoundly. The most significant change occurred in the mid-nineteenth century. Table 3.4 shows the changing employment patterns between the years 1851 and 1871. During this twenty-year period agricultural employment declined by one quarter, while employment in coal mining, iron and steel, machinery and shipbuilding increased by 63%, 101% and 115% respectively. By 1901 fewer than 1 in 10 of the population were employed in agriculture, whereas one third were engaged in manufacturing. Associated with this changing social structure was a growth in income for the lower classes, both relatively and absolutely. There was, however, still much poverty.

A necessary part of the industrialising process was the urbanisation of the British people. Between 1841 and 1911 Britain became a nation of urban dwellers. The population of the towns increased from 8.4 million in 1841 to 23.8 million in 1911, a 182% increase. The areas experiencing the greatest increase were the colliery districts of South Wales, the Midlands, Lancashire, North Yorkshire and the North East of England. The population of these areas rose from 1.3 million to 5.3 million,

Table 3.4   Changes in employment in various economic sectors in Great Britain, 1851–1871 (Source: Teitelbaum, M.S. *The British Fertility Decline*. Copyright © 1984. Reprinted by permission of Princeton University Press)

Sector	1851	1871	Absolute change	% change
Agriculture	1 904 607	1 423 854	−480 753	−25
Coal mining	193 111	315 398	+122 287	+63
Iron & steel	95 350	191 291	+95 941	+101
Machinery & shipbuilding	80 528	172 948	+92 420	+115
Cotton textiles	414 998	508 715	+93 717	+23

a 304% increase, reflecting the changing structure of the economy. At the same time that these changes were taking place in society, England and Wales were experiencing a population explosion. The population increased from an approximate figure of 5.5 million in 1700 to 18 million in 1851. By 1911 the figure had doubled, with a recorded population of 36 million.

The economic status of women during this period was also changing. There was a shift in female employment from the traditional to the modern sectors, particularly in the textile industry. It is estimated that by 1881, two-thirds of the total workforce employed in the textile industry were women. This was to have a significant effect not only on fertility but also mortality, especially infant mortality. With the widespread employment of women, breastfeeding of infants declined markedly, as in many jobs nursing was inconvenient or impossible. Instead, infants were fed on cow's milk and water, now known to be nutritionally inadequate. There was also the danger of disease from unpasteurised milk and contaminated water. It has been estimated that as many as 80% of children who were not breastfed died before the age of one year. This may help to explain why the infant mortality rates for the period, shown in Table 3.5, remained so high.

Despite improvements in the standard of living of most of the British population, there appear to have been counter trends in nutrition. The period 1880 to 1914 was one of improving nutritional standards for a large proportion of the population. For men, the diet in the second half of the nineteenth century improved significantly. Increased quantities of meat, vegetables, bread and sugar were consumed. However, and perhaps more importantly, many women and children, especially of the working classes, were perpetually undernourished. Within the family, food was not shared equally. The women themselves believed that the principal wage earner, usually the man of the household, should receive the nutritionally superior food. As a result, working-class women almost universally suffered from anaemia, general debility and digestive problems. When combined with pregnancy this imposed a severe burden on female health. Under these circumstances prenatal malnutrition was a common occurrence.

Table 3.5   Infant and Child Mortality Rates in England and Wales, 1841–1920 (Source: Teitelbaum, 1984)

Years	Infant mortality per 1000 live births	Mortality of children under 5 years per 1000 living
1841–1850	153	66
1851–1860	154	68
1861–1870	154	69
1871–1880	149	63
1881–1890	142	57
1891–1900	153	58
1901–1910	128	46
1911–1920	100	35

A 40% rejection rate for recruits to the Boer War made it necessary for the authorities to reduce the minimum height for infantrymen from 5'6" (167 cm) to 5'3" (160 cm) in 1883. In 1902 it was further reduced to 5' (152 cm). This situation led to a concerned government establishing an Interdepartmental Committee on Physical Deterioration. This committee was charged with the task of identifying the causes of the poor physique and ill health of much of the population. The report published in 1904 documented the sharp decline in breastfeeding of infants, and the near universal ill health and malnutrition of women, and reported that one-third of children went hungry and most did not get a balanced diet. These factors, it was suggested, explained the poor health of the population.

The sanitary conditions in towns and cities of Britain in the early nineteenth century were poor. Outbreaks of cholera occurred in 1831-2, 1848-9, 1854 and 1866-7. These epidemics, combined with increasing deaths from typhus, led to the Public Health Act of 1848, which had the power to establish local public health authorities upon request or in areas with excessive increases in the death rate. Because of major improvements in the sanitary conditions of larger cities, the death rate fell, for example between 1871-81 the death rate in Birmingham fell from 25.2 per 1000 to 20.7 per 1000. However, it is impossible to calculate how much of this decline was the result of sanitary reforms. In the same period living standards, diet and health care facilities were also improving. It does seem clear, though, that sanitary reforms and rising living standards made a positive impact on

Plate 3.3   This etching of the Fleet Sewer, London, shows repair work being undertaken in 1854. The picture demonstrates the huge engineering feat of the early sanitation engineers. So large and well constructed were these urban sewers that many are still successfully operating beneath our cities today. (Photograph: Mary Evans Picture Library)

mortality decline in cities in the nineteenth century. McKeown puts the contribution at 75% of the decline.

Changes in the character of infectious diseases occur continuously and although related to the environment occur independently of influences such as medical measures, improved hygiene and improved nutrition. McKeown attributed a quarter of the mortality decline in England and Wales during the latter part of that century to the changing character of diseases. Half of this he attributes to changes in scarlet fever. Influenza is another disease whose severity has fluctuated. Similarly, the fatalities from tuberculosis and measles have declined substantially, a decline that began long before any successful medical treatment was discovered.

McKeown dismisses the impact of medical advances and health care on declining mortality rates in England and Wales in the late nineteenth century. But their importance should not be underestimated. The number of doctors practising in England and Wales was steadily increasing, but there were great regional and local variations in the ratio of doctors to population. In London in 1861 the ratio was 1:514, whereas in Wales it was 1:1769. In 1886, the ratios were 1:726 in Brighton, 1:939 in London, 1:2593 in Sheffield and 1:3908 in Salford. Hospital care was provided through Poor Law institutions, especially the workhouses, and after 1868 by infirmaries. There were also voluntary hospitals. These hospitals were founded by private individuals and were maintained by voluntary contributions, from which they derive their name. One of the earliest of these hospitals was the Westminster Hospital (1719), to be followed by others in London such as Guy's Hospital (1725) and the Middlesex Hospital (1745). The first voluntary hospital to be opened outside London was the Winchester Hospital (1736), followed by the Exeter Hospital (1741). By 1861 there were about 900 hospitals in England and Wales, of which approximately 650 could better be described as workhouses. By 1891 the number had risen to 1661, of which 713 were Poor Law institutions. But to what extent was hospital care beneficial? It is difficult to obtain data on this point, but it is generally accepted that hospital care did not increase the mortality rate and may have made a contribution in reducing it, if only by isolating infectious cases.

By the end of the century changes were occurring in medical care. The workers were using their political power to fight for better facilities, the elite saw the need to have healthy workers to ensure the continuance of the Empire and there was also a growing lobby for active intervention by the state in respect to health care. These pressures helped to establish the school meals programme in 1906 and the medical inspection of children entering elementary school. Such changes paved the way for the establishment of a National Health Service almost forty years later.

Although better medicine and health care did not make a direct impact on mortality decline in nineteenth-century England and Wales, they did contribute in other ways. For example, greater awareness of the need for improved health encouraged further public health measures to be taken, and health education to be seen as important. By the end of the century there was a recognisable concept of good health, rather than a negative concept of absence of ill-health. It was this positive approach that led to the setting up of a National Health Insurance scheme in 1911 and the Ministry of Health in 1919, both of which were forerunners of the 1948 National Health Service.

2. Mortality decline in the Third World, the case of Guyana

At the beginning of this century, life expectancy at birth throughout Africa, Asia and Latin America was only 23-28 years. By 1987, the average figure for the three continents had doubled to 62 years. This is still 12 years below the average for the developed world. Within the Third World there are differences: Figure 3.1 shows a life expectation gradation from Latin America through Asia to Africa, which may be equated with a comparable gradation in economic development. But the extent of mortality decline in some countries which have achieved only modest economic growth suggests that factors other than economic development have contributed to the reduction. There is a dispute amongst researchers as to the cause of mortality decline in the Third World. Some argue that it is the result of social and economic development, for example, increased standards of nutrition, housing, water supply and medical care. Others argue that technical changes and innovations such as immunisation, vector eradication and chemotherapy have all had an important part to play. Medical and public health programmes introduced by colonial and more recently by newly independent governments, supported by WHO and other agencies, have also been very important in reducing disease in the Third World. This is a situation quite different from that experienced by Western Europe in the eighteenth and nineteenth centuries when, as we have seen, medical developments played little part in mortality decline. The example of smallpox eradication illustrates the potential of externally derived health programmes. Until the 1960s, smallpox was endemic in much of the inter-tropical world. In 1966, WHO intensified its campaign against the disease, principally by the widespread use of vaccination programmes, and by 1980 the disease had been eliminated.

The technical solution to the problem of achieving mortality reduction is the importation of western chemical innovations, without associated socio-economic improvements. This method has been applied in many Third World countries with often spectacular and well documented results, for example in Sri Lanka and

Plate 3.4 Immunisation campaigns are an important way of reducing child mortality. These posters were part of the 1989 Moroccan polio vaccination campaign.
(Photograph: H.R. Barrett)

(a)

(b)

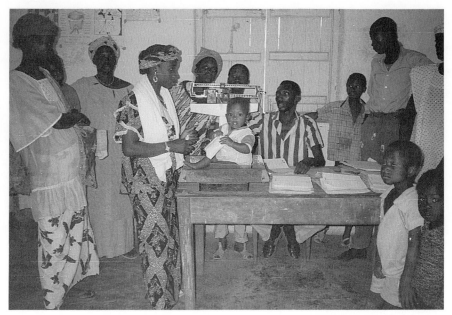

Plate 3.5 The monitoring of babies and toddlers at maternal and childcare clinics can help reduce infant mortality. At this rural clinic in West Africa a baby is being weighed by the local health worker. (Photograph: A.W. Browne)

Plate 3.6 The provision of safe, clean water is an important part of mortality control. Here in The Gambia in West Africa, the Saudi Sahelian Project is providing villages with sealed hand or foot pumped wells. (Photograph: H.R. Barrett)

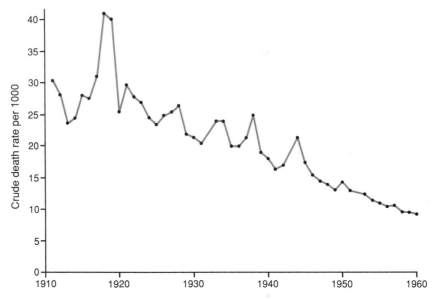

Figure 3.11   Crude death rates in Guyana (British Guiana), 1911–1960 (Source: compiled from Mandle, 1970)

Mauritius. A similar success story is found in Guyana, a small state in Latin America with an area of only 215 000 square kilometres. Guyana was formerly the British colony known as British Guiana. The death rate statistics for the colony from 1911 to 1960 are shown in Figure 3.11. From this graph it can be seen that the CDR in 1911 was 30 per 1000. In 1929 and 1930 the CDR fell to below 24 and from 1929 to 1940 the colony experienced fluctuating death rates, but showed a generally downward trend, with an average for the period of 22 per 1000. That is a 25% reduction on the previous period. In 1939 the CDR fell below 20 for the first time and thereafter mortality declined steadily, with the exception of 1944, reaching a low of 9 per 1000 in 1960. The rate of improvement in the death rate has been particularly noticeable since 1945.

Throughout the period 1911-1960 five groups of diseases were the principal causes of death in Guyana. They were malaria and undefined fever; pneumonia and bronchitis; diarrhoea and enteritis; tuberculosis; and kidney disease (which is associated with numerous malarial attacks). In the period 1911-1928 these diseases accounted for 50% of the colony's mortality. In the period 1929-1940 this declined slightly to 47%. In the early 1940s these diseases accounted for 40-45% of mortality, but by 1960 accounted for only 26% of deaths. In other words from 1911 to 1960 these diseases accounted for 60% of the mortality decline. Throughout the period 1911-1945 malaria stood out as the single most important cause of death. After 1945 the pattern changed abruptly, until by 1960 malaria was virtually insignificant.

The high death rates in Guyana in the period 1911-1929 are associated with overcrowding and poor sanitary conditions and the fact that the coastal plain was below sea level, providing an excellent breeding ground for the mosquito vector of

96

the disease malaria. The breeding grounds for mosquitoes were unintentionally enlarged by the establishment of irrigation schemes along the coast. However, after 1929 death rates began to decline. Some researchers have argued that the decline was due to rising living standards, but in the case of Guyana this seems unlikely.

Guyana was basically an agricultural colony producing sugar and rice. The period 1911-1940 was a period of economic stagnation when export earnings from sugar declined. Living standards are unlikely to have risen in the colony during this period. From 1940-1960 there is evidence that economic stagnation continued, with daily food intake per capita actually declining, both in terms of calorific and protein intake. Under these conditions it seems unlikely that economic conditions contributed to mortality reduction.

There is, however, much evidence to suggest that public health programmes did contribute to mortality decline. The colony's first Medical Office of Health was created in 1911 and efforts were concentrated on clearing drains and removing waste from the capital, Georgetown. In the period after 1918 water supplies were improved by the successful implementation of an artesian well digging programme. Malaria was the object of a number of special programmes. Before 1945 these took the form of eliminating the mosquito's breeding area by filling in swamps, clearing bush from around villages and treating latrines with carbolic oil. After 1945 the DDT campaign was begun, which involved periodically spraying the breeding grounds of mosquitoes with what we now know to be a very dangerous insecticide. These measures, in particular the DDT campaign, were very successful and have been credited with accounting for over 40% of the mortality decline, due to the reduced number of deaths from malaria and kidney disease.

In Guyana from 1911 to 1960 it is clear that public health improvements and not economic advances were responsible for mortality decline. The post-Second World War DDT campaign is clearly the most important reason for mortality decline, but improving health education, medical facilities, water supplies and waste disposal should not be dismissed.

Guyana is not alone in the Third World in recording large successes in reducing death rates in the period up to the mid-1960s, but since then mortality decline in many parts of the Third World has slowed down. This implies that the technical solution, including low cost public health measures such as mass vaccination programmes and DDT spraying campaigns, achieves limited results. Without the accompanying socio-economic improvements in nutrition, safe water supplies and access to education, employment and health care facilities, the technical solution loses momentum. Research in Latin America indicates that malnutrition is now the primary cause of, or major contributory factor, towards 60% of child mortality. Those particularly at risk are the landless rural population, the urban poor, and particularly women and children. The evidence points to the fact that the major killer in the Third World today is poverty. This can be solved only by socio-political strategies that explicitly emphasise improvement of the social welfare of the population at large. This is why countries such as Cuba, China, Vietnam, Sri Lanka and Nicaragua, where social programmes are at the forefront of development efforts, have mortality and fertility levels well below countries with comparable GNP per head.

3. Age-sex differentials in mortality: the case of India

Age and sex structures are key factors in mortality patterns, with the mortality of males exceeding that of females at almost every age and in almost every country. This results in higher life expectancy rates for females. Only in five countries do life expectancies for men exceed those for women. These countries are Bangladesh, Bhutan, India, Nepal and Pakistan, all in Southern Asia. Reasons for this reversal will be explored below.

Differentials in mortality by sex can be explained by the continuous interaction of environmental and socio-economic factors. The lower levels of mortality of one sex may be explained by biological superiority, or be the result of lower exposure to hazardous factors. Whatever the reasons the evidence suggests that the female of the human species lives longer than the male.

A notable exception to this pattern is observable in India, where male life expectancy at birth currently exceeds female life expectancy. It has been suggested that female survival rates are a direct indicator of the relative status of women within society. In regions and households where women are likely to play an economically more active role, the family has a stronger incentive to invest in girls to assure its own survival.

India began to experience a sustained decline in mortality in the late 1920s and 1930s, following the severe influenza epidemic of 1918-1921. Male life expectancy at birth was estimated at 27 years in the period 1921-1930 and had increased to 57 years by 1986. Life expectancy for women in 1986 was a year less at 56 years. This is due to the higher death rates experienced by females of all age groups, which is in total contrast to the demographic patterns of mortality in other parts of the world. This inequality in death rates between the sexes is best illustrated using the *sex ratio index*, which is the number of males per 100 females. The male-female child survival ratio is about 104 in India, whereas it is approximately 95 for most industrially advanced countries.

By analysing the state level sex ratio statistics for India, shown in Table 3.6, it becomes clear that male ratios are higher in the northern states than in the southern states. When the district level data is mapped as in Figure 3.12 it also becomes clear that the country can be divided in two by a line that approximates to the contours of the Satpura and Chota Nagpur Hills. To the north of this line sex ratios are high, especially in Punjab, Haryana and parts of Uttar Pradesh. To the south, sex ratios are comparatively low. West Bengal clearly fits into this category.

The statistics support the suggestion that the main reason for this variation in sex ratios in India is sex differentials in mortality. Mortality figures for infant and child deaths shown in Table 3.6 illustrate the significant mortality disadvantage suffered by females throughout the northern states. The spatial pattern described has existed for many decades and appears to be the result of socio-cultural variations that are deeply rooted in Indian society.

In northern India, marriage is exogamous, that is women move to their husband's home, sometimes a great distance from their own family home. They also marry young. As shown in Table 3.6 in all but two states the average age at first marriage

Table 3.6 Sex-ratio data and statistics related to female status in India, by state (Source: Dyson & Moore, 1983)

	Population 1981 '000s	Sex ratio (males per 100 females) 1901	1961	1981	Ratio of male to female infant and child mortality 1971	Female labour force particip- ation rate 1971 %	Women in seclusion %	Women literate %	Female age at first marriage 1971	Total fertility rate
South										
Kerala	25 403	99	98	97	95	13	4.3	54.3	20.9	5.43
Tamil Nadu	48 297	96	101	102	95	15	4.9	26.9	19.6	4.97
Andhra Pradesh	58 404	101	102	103	90	24	9.4	15.7	16.4	4.88
Karanataka	37 043	102	104	104	93	14	5.4	20.9	17.9	5.68
Maharashtra	62 694	102	107	107	102	20	16.7	26.4	17.5	5.16
North										
Gujarat	33 961	105	106	106	110	10	41.8	24.7	18.3	6.19
Rajasthan	34 103	110	110	109	115	8	62.2	8.5	15.4	6.32
Uttar Pradesh	110 858	107	110	113	136	7	46.4	10.7	15.6	6.85
Madhya Pradesh	52 132	101	105	106	103	19	42.9	10.9	15.2	6.38
Punjab	16 670	120	117	113	138	1	44.6	25.9	20.1	6.32
Haryana	12 851	116	116	114	124	2	72.6	14.9	16.6	6.68
East										
Bihar	69 823	95	101	106	106	9	29.6	8.7	15.5	5.01
West Bengal	54 486	106	114	110	101	4	na	22.4	17.8	4.42
Orissa	26 272	96	100	102	87	7	27.7	13.9	17.2	5.65
All India	683 810	103	106	107	109	12	na	18.7	17.2	5.78

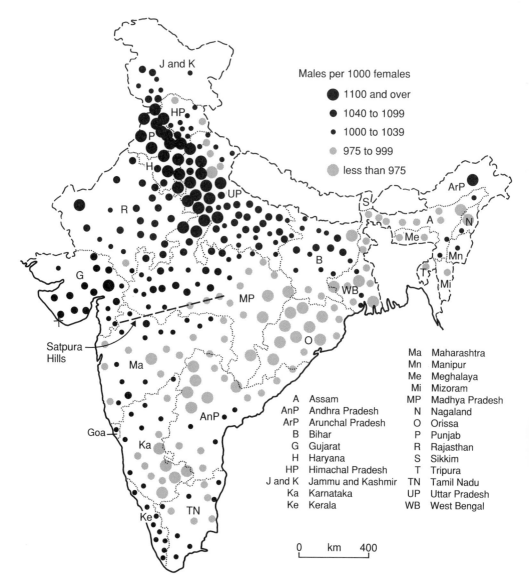

Figure 3.12 Sex ratios for children aged 0–9 years, by district in India, 1961 (Source: Dyson and Moore, 1983)

is below the national average of 17.2 years. This also perhaps explains the fact that fertility in these states is well above the national average of 5.78. The dowry is the main marriage transaction, putting financial pressure on the parents of girls, and because women are out-marriers, parents can expect little help from their daughters after marriage. The sexuality of females in northern India is rigidly controlled, where from 40–70% of women observe rules of seclusion. Because of social control, female formal employment is low in northern India and may involve interaction only with other women. Women are not major contributors to the household food budget, since the staple in this region is wheat, a crop grown by men and requiring little female labour. Females are therefore of little economic value in northern India and this is reflected in low female literacy rates. Females in northern India have little autonomy and consequently have a low status in society. The fact that females traditionally have little labour value and marriage costs for daughters are high may help explain the adverse sex ratio in these areas.

It would appear therefore that the high female child mortality rate in the north is strongly influenced by age-old practices of discrimination against females with particular regard to access to food and medical care. There are historical references to female infanticide in northwestern India. The reasons for this gender discrimination is related to the northern Indian culture where patrilineal descent is central to social organisation, as is the production of sons.

In southern India the situation is rather different. The most common form of marriage is local cross-cousin marriage and therefore does not necessarily involve the female moving long distances. This enables women to help their parents in old age and makes it feasible for them to inherit property rights. Bridewealth is the most common form of marriage agreement, and female age at first marriage is higher than the national average, which may also account for the lower than average fertility rate. In southern India female movements are less controlled and fewer women are in seclusion. In turn women are more economically active with a higher average labour force participation rate and a correspondingly higher literacy rate. It is clear that females in southern India have a higher economic value than females in the north as they are the main suppliers of labour to grow rice, the staple food of the region. As a result they enjoy greater freedom than their counterparts in the north. The greater economic value of women to the household in southern India may account for the more favourable sex ratio in this part of India.

The brief discussion above points to the fact that female social and economic status is probably the single most important element in explaining low female life expectancy as compared to males in India, and the correspondingly adverse sex ratios experienced in northern India.

4. Age-sex specific mortality increase in Hungary since 1970

Contrary to the experience in other European countries, the death rate in Eastern Europe has experienced a dramatic deterioration in the last twenty years. Crude death rates have risen substantially in Bulgaria, Poland, Romania, Czechoslovakia and Hungary as well as in the USSR. This increase is not only a function of an ageing population, but a real increase in the mortality rates of certain groups, particularly of men aged 35-59. In only two Eastern European countries, East Germany and Yugoslavia, were death rates for this group lower in 1978 than in 1965. In the corresponding group of women in these countries the decline in the mortality rate has slowed down and in Hungary and Bulgaria it is now increasing. These trends are very different from the pattern evident in contemporary Western Europe. These trends in East European mortality appear to have gone farthest in

Plate 3.7   A heavy smog lies over the city of Leipzig in the former territory of East Germany. Environmental experts estimate that over $119 billion is needed to repair the damage to the environment caused by its industry. Such pollution has inevitably contributed to increasing mortality levels in Eastern Europe. (Photograph: Popperfoto)

Hungary. In 1961 out of the 25 major countries of Europe, Hungary ranked 15 in terms of crude death rate, above Austria, Belgium, UK, France, Ireland, East and West Germany, Portugal and Sweden; by 1981 Hungary had the highest death rate in Europe after East Germany.

The historical decline in Hungarian mortality began in the 1880s and apart from temporary increases associated with the two world wars was maintained until the 1960s. Mortality reached its lowest point in 1961 when the death rate was recorded as 9.6 per 1000. However, since the mid 1960s, the annual death totals have increased annually from 102 000 in 1966 to 145 000 in 1981, a rise of over 40%. Correspondingly the crude death rate has increased from 10.0 to 13.5 per 1000 in the same period. Part of this rise is the result of an ageing population. Between 1960 and 1980 the number of people aged over 60 increased by 33%, and those aged over 75 by 75%. Total population increase in the same period was only 7.5%. Although there is a pronounced ageing of the Hungarian population, it is of the same general magnitude as other countries in Europe. It therefore appears that there must be a rise in the real level of mortality, in order to explain the increasing death rate.

By looking at the data in more detail it becomes obvious that there is a difference in the death rates between the sexes. Figure 3.13 shows that the standardised death rate for women has remained virtually static since 1966, ranging from 9.5 to 10.1 per 1000. Ninety per cent of the rise in the female death rate can be attributed to ageing. The figures for men are very different. The mortality rate for Hungarian males is one of the highest in Europe (exceeded only by Yugoslavia and Portugal).

102

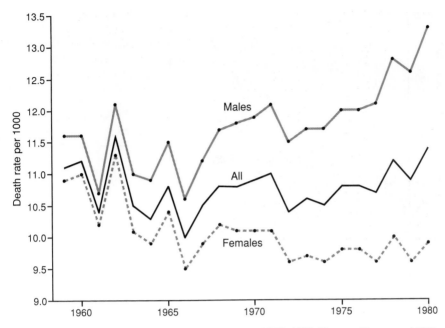

Figure 3.13   Standardised Death Rates in Hungary, 1959–1980 (Source: Compton, 1985)

It is also exceptional in its large increase in recent years. The age-specific death rates shown in Figure 3.14 illustrate a complex pattern.

Although male middle-aged mortality is rising in other European countries Hungary is exceptional in that the percentage increase is the highest. This trend is especially noticeable in men aged 35-59 for whom mortality has increased by 68% between 1966 and 1980. It is even more noticeable in the category of men aged 45-59 where there has been a 90% increase. Death rates for women show a similar trend, increasing by 22% in the 35-59 age group, and by 33% in the 45-59 age category. This fairly substantial rise in death rates for middle-aged women in Hungary is unique within Europe. In other European countries the rates are either static or declining.

Analysing cause of death data can help explain these recent mortality trends. It is clear that the principal causes of death in Hungary conform to the pattern observed elsewhere in Europe. Heart disease is the cause of most deaths, followed by cancer and diseases of the circulatory system. But there are some cause-specific death rates which have increased substantially as a proportion of the total. These are bronchitis, diabetes and acute liver disease. Deaths from infectious diseases, pneumonia and influenza have declined in relative significance. Figure 3.15 shows that most of the increase in the death rate can be attributed to the combined impact of diseases of the circulatory system and cancer. For men more than half the increase in the death rate between 1966 and 1981 is attributable to diseases of the circulatory system, followed in order of importance by deaths from cancer, respiratory disease, injuries and poisoning and diseases of the digestive system.

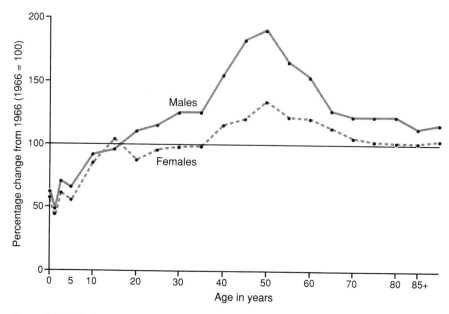

Figure 3.14   Hungary: Age specific death rates by sex in 1980 as a percentage of the corresponding rates in 1966 (Source: data from Compton, 1985)

Figure 3.15   Hungary: percentage changes in the cause of death by sex, 1966–1980 (1966 = 100) (Source: data from Compton, 1985)

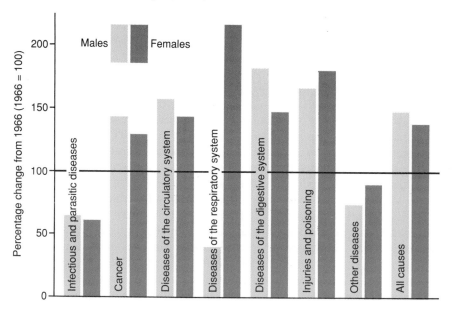

Diseases of the circulatory system also accounted for the majority of the increase in the deaths of women in the same period.

The next question to be answered is why there has been this rise in age and sex-selective mortality in Hungary since 1966. A number of possible explanations await further research. It is suggested that the transformation of Hungarian society since 1950, with the introduction of new life styles, has increased a number of mortality risks. The most notable of these changes is the rapid pace of urbanisation and industrialisation. Supporting this explanation is the fact that the mortality rate of manual workers is 50% higher than members of cooperative farms. Associated with this societal change is the increase in leisure time and disposable incomes, which has resulted in rising car ownership, increased alcohol consumption and cigarette smoking. Of particular concern to the authorities is the consumption of alcohol, which is strongly associated with assaults, suicides, traffic fatalities and cirrhosis of the liver. The size of the problem is indicated by the fact that the consumption of spirits rose from six million litres in 1970 to 22 million litres in 1978. Hungarians now spend on average nearly 12% of their disposable income on alcohol. Other factors which may help account for the rise in mortality are the associations between certain forms of cancer and the inhalation of asbestos dust and vinylchloride gas used in manufacturing processes. In the 1950s there was widespread use of chest x-rays in Hungary before the realisation that this may be linked to breast cancer in women. Some specialists have even blamed the Hungarian diet, which has a high fat content, low fibre and vegetable content, combined with high alcohol intake.

Whatever the causes, it is clear that the death rate in Hungary and other East European countries will continue to rise, if only because of the continued ageing of the population. A death rate of between 14.0 and 14.5 per 1000 is predicted for Hungary in the late 1990s, to be compared with 12 per 1000 for UK and 9 per 1000 for Spain.

ASSIGNMENTS

1. How does the experience of mortality decline in twentieth-century Guyana differ from that of nineteenth-century England and Wales?

2. (a) Using Figure 3.12 as a base map and the data from Table 3.6, draw four choropleth maps of the following information:
  i) the ratio of male to female infant and child mortality rates;
  ii) percentage of women in seclusion;
  iii) female labour force participation rates;
  iv) percentage of literate women.

  (b) Describe the patterns shown.

  (c) Compare your maps with Figure 3.12. What do the five maps tell us about the status of women and female life expectancy in India?

3. (a) At which stage of the Demographic Transition is Hungary? Justify your answer.

  (b) At what stage of the Epidemiological Transition is Hungary (use Figure 3.15)?

  (c) Account for the role of environmental and socio-economic factors in Hungary's mortality experience.

Key Ideas

Introduction

1. Mortality is an important component of population change.
2. Mortality can be measured in a number of ways: crude death rates, standardised death rates and life expectancy at birth.

A. Geography of mortality

1. World variations in mortality are smaller than variations in fertility.
2. There are spatial variations, with Africa experiencing the highest CDRs and Japan and China experiencing the lowest CDRs.

B. Causes of mortality

1. Causes of mortality can be attributed to environmental factors and socio-economic factors.
2. The relative importance of these factors produce differences in the causes of mortality between the developed and developing countries.

C. Causes of mortality decline

1. Mortality decline can be attributed to the interplay of four factors: sanitary reforms, changing disease patterns, improved medicine and healthcare, and improvements in living standards.
2. Sanitary reforms can reduce mortality by eliminating the environmental conditions under which diseases are spread.
3. Mortality may decrease due to the changing character of infectious diseases.
4. Improved medicine and healthcare had a debatable impact on nineteenth-century mortality levels. They have been very important since the development of chemotherapy in the 1940s.
5. Premature mortality levels decrease with rising living standards, particularly with adequate nutrition.

D. Case Studies

1. McKeown presents a model to explain mortality decline in the second half of the nineteenth century in England and Wales.
2. He attributes this decline to the changing character of some diseases, the introduction of sanitary reform measures and higher standards of living.
3. Medical and healthcare facilities had little impact on the mortality patterns of England and Wales until the middle of the twentieth century.
4. Mortality declines in the Third World since 1900 can be attributed to the importation of innovations such as vaccinations, vector eradication programmes and chemotherapy.

Table 3.7 Infant Mortality Rates, immunisation rates, access to safe water, daily calorie supply and female literacy levels for 20 selected developing countries (Source: data from UNDP, 1990)

		Infant mortality rate per 1000 live births 1988	One-year olds immunised 1987 %	Population with access to safe water 1985–87 %	Daily calorie supply as % of requirements 1984–86	Adult female literacy rate 1985 %
1	Sierra Leone	153	40	25	81	21
2	Somalia	131	28	34	90	6
3	Bangladesh	118	18	46	83	22
4	Pakistan	108	65	44	97	19
5	Nigeria	104	62	46	90	31
6	India	98	63	57	100	29
7	Côte d' Ivoire	95	37	19	110	31
8	Peru	87	66	55	93	78
9	Indonesia	84	71	38	116	65
10	Egypt	83	85	73	132	30
11	Senegal	80	57	53	99	19
12	Saudi Arabia	70	88	97	125	31
13	Brazil	62	68	78	111	76
14	Iran	61	81	76	138	39
15	Mexico	46	74	77	135	88
16	Thailand	38	79	64	105	88
17	Argentina	32	68	56	136	96
18	Malaysia	24	74	84	121	66
19	Costa Rica	18	89	91	124	93
20	Singapore	9	95	100	124	79

5. The example of Guyana demonstrates how technology can reduce mortality.
6. Without accompanying socio-economic improvements the technical solution will lose its momentum.
7. In contrast to the global experience, life expectancy at birth for females in India is below that for males.
8. This can be explained by higher female mortality, which may be the result of the status of females within Indian society.
9. Contrary to experience in other European countries, the death rate in Eastern Europe has increased in the last twenty years, most notably in Hungary. This is principally the result of high male middle-aged mortality.
10. Reasons suggested for this pattern are the rapid pace of urbanisation and industrialisation of the country since the Second World War, accompanied by increased consumption of alcohol and cigarettes in association with a high fat and low fibre diet.

Additional Activities

1. This activity is suitable only for students who are able to visit a small cemetery or graveyard.
    (a) Visit your local cemetery and note down the sex, age and year of death of the occupants.
    (b) Plot on a scattergraph, for both males and females, age at death and year of death.
    (c) Describe the pattern found and note any differences between the sexes.
2. (a) Using the Spearman's Rank Correlation Coefficient (see below for explanation) and the data given in Table 3.7, correlate Infant Mortality Rates with the following variables:
        i) percentage of one-year olds vaccinated;
        ii) percentage of population with access to safe water;
        iii) daily calorie supply as a percentage of requirements;
        iv) percentage of literate women.
    (b) Complete Table 3.8 and discuss your results.
    (c) What do your results indicate concerning the relative importance of the variables in reducing Infant Mortality Rates in the developing world?

Table 3.8   Correlation co-efficients of Infant Mortality Rate with four selected variables

	Infant mortality rate Spearman's rank correlation coefficient
One year olds immunised Access to safe water Daily calorie supply Female literacy rate	

3. With reference to the Demographic Transition Model described in Chapter 2, discuss the contention that Guyana's mortality decline does not conform to Notestein's model.

Spearman's Rank Correlation Coefficient.

The Spearman's Rank Correlation Coefficient (r_s), calculates a value to show the degree of association between two variables. The values range between 0 and +/- 1.0. Zero indicates no correlation and 1.0 a perfect correlation. The sign attached to the value represents the direction of association. For the statistic to be calculated, the data must first be ranked. The following calculation can then be performed:

$$r_s = 1 - \left(\frac{6 \sum^n d^2}{(n^3 - n)} \right)$$

d = the difference in rank between the two data sets
n = number of paired observations.

---

4 Fertility as a Component of Population Change

Introduction

Low levels of mortality are desired by all societies and reductions can be brought about by public actions such as education and immunisation programmes. Fertility, however, depends on individual decisions. Fertility, which is defined as the measured capacity of a population to generate births, is an extremely complex behavioural puzzle, influenced by numerous factors. Due to the declining levels of mortality experienced by all nations of the world during this century, fertility is now a critical component of population composition and growth. This chapter will examine the principal factors that influence fertility levels and assess their impact on population growth.

The principles and procedures for measuring fertility are very similar to those of mortality discussed in Chapter 3.

(a) The simplest and most commonly used measure is the *crude birth rate* (CBR). This measure consists of dividing the number of births in a given year by the population living in the same territory during that year, and multiplying by 1000. It shows the exact rate at which additions are made to a population through births. However, it is reliant on the accuracy of the data used. In many countries, especially in the Third World, births are not registered and population data may be extremely inaccurate. The one major disadvantage of the CBR is that it does not take into account the age and sex structure of the population. Thus a population with a high proportion of elderly people may appear to have a low CBR, when in fact the number of children born to women in their reproductive years may be high.

(b) Other fertility measures attempt to standardise for the variable age and sex composition of the population, so that births are related specifically to the number of women in their reproductive period. The *total fertility rate* measures the number of children that would be born to 1000 women passing through the child bearing ages, assuming that none of the women die during this period. This index is one of the most sensitive and meaningful cross sectional measures of fertility, and when expressed as fertility rates *per woman*, enables direct comparisons to be made with other populations. The *total fertility rate per woman* is also useful in indicating the replacement level of the population. A total fertility rate of 2.1 births per woman is the level of fertility widely accepted as indicating a stable population, i.e. the rate which is necessary to replace both parents. A rate greater than 2.1 indicates a growing population and a rate smaller than 2.1 a declining population. To many demographers this is a critical measure of the growth of a population. In 1988, twenty eight countries in the world had fertility rates per woman of less than 2.1, including Hong Kong, Singapore, Yugoslavia, and many countries in the Western world.

A. Geography of Fertility

Crude birth rates as illustrated in Figure 4.1 portray a very complex spatial pattern. Western and Eastern Africa report the highest CBRs of 49 per 1000, followed by Central Africa with 45 per 1000. In contrast the lowest rate of 12 is recorded for Western Europe, followed by Northern Europe and Japan, both with a recorded CBR of 13 per 1000. However, within these regions there are large national variations. The highest CBRs of over 50 per 1000 are to be found in the African countries of Malawi (53), Rwanda (52), Kenya (52) and Niger (51), whilst the lowest CBRs of less than 12 per 1000 occur in Europe, the lowest being former West Germany (10), Denmark (11), Austria (11) and Greece (11).

Fertility rates (see Figure 4.2) show a similar pattern. Seven African countries record a fertility rate of over 7 children per woman, including the three countries with the highest global fertility rates, Rwanda (8.0), Kenya (7.7) and Malawi (7.6). At the other end of the scale there are seven countries with fertility rates of less than 1.5. These are all in Europe, where the former territory of West Germany scored the lowest global fertility rate of 1.3, followed by Denmark with 1.4.

Although there is a wide variation in CBRs and fertility rates, since 1965 there have been significant decreases in CBRs in many parts of the world. The greatest decreases have occurred in China (a decrease of 19 per 1000 in the CBR), Cuba (18), Colombia (18) and Mauritius (17). In fact, since 1965 all but 17 countries have experienced a fertility decline, a decline that is particularly noticeable in China, North Africa, Central America, South America and South East Asia. It is perhaps significant that all the countries registering an increase in fertility in the last twenty years are in Africa. This could have serious implications for the future economic development of that continent.

B. Factors affecting Fertility

There are clearly very wide spatial variations in global fertility patterns, and although fertility rates are falling in several Asian and many Latin American countries, the rates for Africa are continuing to rise. It is important, therefore, for the population geographer to determine which factors may be responsible for fertility trends. Most demographers recognise three inter-connected sets of factors which affect fertility rates:

1. biological factors, commonly referred to as the *proximate determinants* of fertility;

111

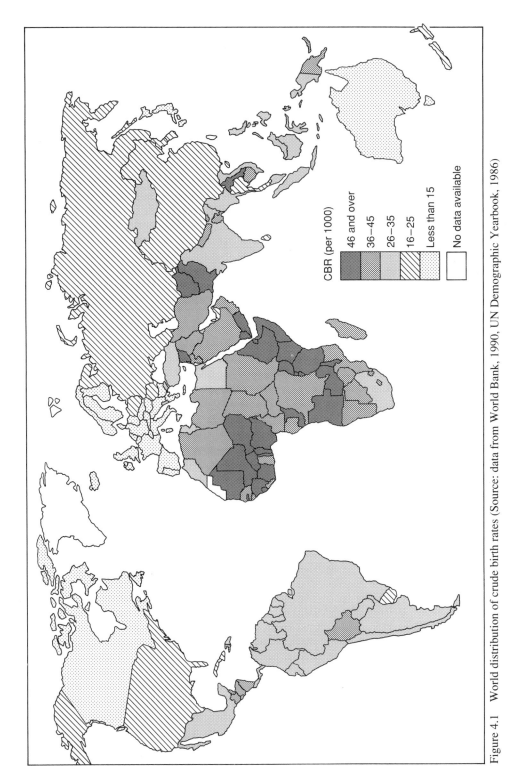

Figure 4.1 World distribution of crude birth rates (Source: data from World Bank, 1990, UN Demographic Yearbook, 1986)

CBR (per 1000)

46 and over

36–45

26–35

16–25

Less than 15

No data available

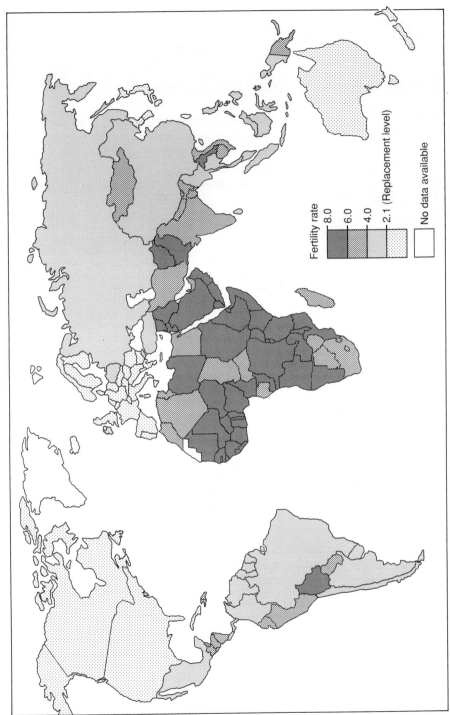

Figure 4.2   World distribution of fertility rates (Source: data from World Bank, 1990, UN Demographic Yearbook, 1986)

2. socio-economic factors;
3. institutional intervention.

1. Proximate determinants (biological factors)

Fertility levels are entirely determined by trends in the proximate determinants of a population. In contrast, socio-economic factors can affect fertility only indirectly, by modifying the proximate determinants. A review of the biological and behavioural factors that comprise the proximate determinants will demonstrate their importance in affecting fertility levels. Proximate determinants include: marriage patterns; patterns of sexual activity; duration of breastfeeding; the number of induced abortions; levels of sterility; and the percentage of couples using contraception.

(a) Marriage patterns

This determinant assesses the degree to which women of reproductive age are exposed to the risk of conceiving. In theory a woman can bear children throughout her reproductive life, which on average begins during the teenage years and is completed by the mid-forties. In practice a woman is rarely at risk for this length of time, because her exposure to childbearing is limited to the amount of that time in which she is actively involved in a sexual relationship, usually referred to as marriage.

In much of the Third World the average age at which women marry has risen since the turn of the century, a pattern observed in parts of Europe during the late nineteenth century. In India, for example, the average age at which women marry has risen from thirteen years in the 1920s to seventeen years by the 1980s (the comparable figures for men being twenty and twenty-two years). The incidence of child marriage in India has also declined. In 1901 a quarter of all ten to fourteen-year-old girls were married; by 1921 this had fallen to 20%. In 1951, only 5% of all girls in this age group were married and in the 1980s, although against the law, it is estimated that 1% of girls of this age group were married. There is also evidence of a difference between the two main religious groups. Rural Hindu women marry earlier than rural Muslim women, a situation that is reversed in urban areas. Age at marriage is higher for urban women, the average difference between urban and rural areas being 2.5 years. This is also a trend common in most developing countries.

Although it is accepted that age at marriage for women is increasing, marriage patterns do vary. In South Asia and sub-Saharan Africa over 50% of women aged between fifteen and nineteen years are married; in Latin America the number is less than 20% and in Korea and Hong Kong the proportion is only 5%. The age at marriage of women is a function of women's status and economic role within society, which is often associated with the stage of economic development of a nation. This will be discussed later in this chapter.

Age is not the only factor associated with marriage which should be considered. The proportion of women who never marry, the frequency of divorce, widowhood

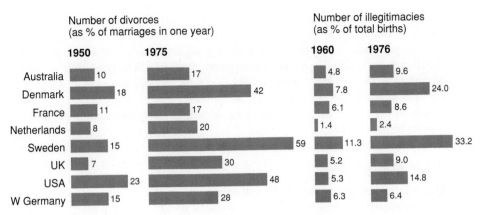

Figure 4.3 Number of divorces and illegitimate births in eight developed countries
(Source: New Internationalist, December 1982)

and remarriage and the social acceptability of illegitimate children can all affect
fertility levels. These factors are gaining importance, particularly in the developed
world. Figure 4.3 shows the number of divorces and number of illegitimate births,
both of which are increasing, in eight developed countries. Research continues to
assess the impact of such trends on fertility patterns.

(b) Patterns of sexual activity

This determinant directly affects the probability of conceiving among ovulating
(egg-producing) women. Within marriage exposure to pregnancy depends on the
pattern of sexual activity. The three most important factors being: frequency of
intercourse; patterns of sexual abstinence; and separation of spouses.

i) *Frequency of intercourse.* There is strong evidence that differences in coital
frequency are associated with marriage forms. Women in polygamous marriages in
general have a lower fertility than monogamously married women. Lower frequency
of intercourse (of each woman) is one of the main explanations. In a polygamous
marriage, which is common in many Islamic societies, a man may have more than
one wife at any time and as a result time spent with the husband is shared amongst
the wives. But fertility in polygamous unions may be lower for other reasons: men
may take a second wife if their first wife is infertile; and polygamy facilitates the
practice of prolonged abstinence from sexual relations while a newborn baby is
breastfeeding. This practice, which is technically known as *postpartum abstinence*,
is common in many societies, but especially in sub-Saharan Africa. Patterns in
Africa show considerable variations. Reported sexual abstinence of forty days or
more are to be found in the lake regions of Eastern Central Africa and in scattered
parts of the Sahel and South Eastern Africa. Durations of up to one year occur in
Eastern Africa and Ghana, but the longest length of abstinence, of over two years,
is found throughout sub-Sahelien Africa and Central Africa.

ii) *Spousal separation.* Long periods of separation between couples can appreciably
reduce a woman's overall exposure to conception. Such separations are principally

115

the result of labour migration, but the effect on fertility levels depends on the timing of the move. In some areas husbands leave to find work once their wives become pregnant, and remain away during the early years of the child's life, therefore re-enforcing the custom of postpartum abstinence. The large-scale migration of men to work in South Africa probably explains the long duration of abstinence reported in South Eastern Africa. In other areas the movement of young unmarried people in the search for work may well delay the age of first marriage and thus depress fertility levels.

(c) Length of breastfeeding

This determinant affects fertility by delaying the onset of ovulation and menstruation after a birth. Breastfeeding lengthens a woman's period of natural infertility after a birth by effectively blocking ovulation, and can therefore increase the interval before the woman can conceive again. It is a natural mechanism designed to protect the health and well-being of both mother and child. Breastfeeding is common practice in many Third World countries, especially Southern Asia and sub-Saharan Africa, and has thus depressed fertility rates in these areas. But there is mounting evidence that many countries have experienced declines in the average duration of breastfeeding. In Thailand, for example, between 1969 and 1979 the average duration of breastfeeding in urban areas fell from 12.9 months to 8.4 months, and in Taiwan the average fell from 14.6 to 8.8 months in the period 1966-1980. Other countries, particularly in South East Asia and Latin America, have also reported marked declines. This reduction in the length of the breastfeeding period tends to increase potential fertility and is due to two factors: i) the opportunity and ii) the motivation of mothers to breastfeed their offspring.

Plate 4.1   Rural women in West Africa breastfeed their children in the fields. Motherhood does not preclude them from being agriculturally active. (Photograph: H.R. Barrett)

i) *Opportunity to breastfeed.* The opportunity to breastfeed babies is dependent on the ability of the mother to combine nursing with her other roles in society, particularly her economic role. In many parts of Africa for instance, women are the major producers of food crops and are thus able to combine their roles of mother and farmer by taking their babies to the fields with them, where they may stop and feed the child as necessary. However, in societies where women are engaged in economic activity outside their homes, in the formal economic sector such as in offices or factories, it is inconvenient, if not impossible, for women to nurse children during working hours and the baby may be left with a minder and fed with powdered milk (see paragraph (ii) below). Increasing industrialisation and economic development can be seen to be a major contributory factor in the decline of the length of time many children are breastfed.

ii) *Motivation to breastfeed.* The motivation to breastfeed is a reflection of prevailing fashions in infant feeding and of advice given by the health professions. In the 1960s and 1970s it was fashionable in many Third World countries to feed babies with powdered milk. This was partly the result of aggressive advertising by the manufacturers and the desire of many mothers to appear *modern* or *westernised.* Unfortunately many of these mothers did not have access to pure water, did not understand the need for stringent hygiene of feeding equipment and very often could not read the instructions on how to mix the powder. The result was high infant mortality rates and increased incidence of malnutrition in young children who had been fed with artificial milk. Since the beginning of the 1980s the health problems associated with artificial feeding methods have been recognised by the medical profession and world bodies such as UNICEF and the World Health Organisation (WHO), and there have been active campaigns to promote the benefits to both mother and child of breastfeeding. However, despite these campaigns reduced periods of breastfeeding have had, and will continue to have, a large impact on fertility.

(d) Induced abortion

This determinant includes any practice that deliberately interrupts the normal course of gestation. Irrespective of legal status, induced abortion is practised in almost every country around the globe. Any practice of this type has a direct impact upon fertility, but it is difficult to obtain data on this very controversial subject, even in countries where abortion is legal. A number of countries, most notably in Eastern Europe, have used induced abortion as the main method of population control and its impact on fertility levels has been marked. The use of induced abortion to control fertility is discussed in the case study in Chapter 6.

(e) Sterility

Sterility is the inability to conceive or carry a child. This may be the result of infertility in one or both partners. Sterility arises from both natural and disease-related (pathological) causes.

i) *Natural sterility*. Natural infertility of women in most populations is approximately 3% at the age of twenty and increases with age, until at the age of about fifty it is universal. The causes of natural sterility are usually chromosomal or congenital in nature. Treatment is expensive and rarely successful. For this reason eradication of natural sterility is unlikely to occur in the near future and thus will have little impact on future fertility levels.

ii) *Pathological sterility*. Pathological sterility is the result of infections. In women the main causes of this type of infertility are gonorrhoea and infections that are the result of illegal abortion practices. Most of these infections, if identified in their early stages, can be successfully treated by modern medicine. This has important implications for fertility levels in countries where pathological sterility is prevalent.

The incidence of pathological sterility can be reduced successfully by a combination of educational programmes, medical treatment and access to contraception, which should reduce the need for dangerous illegal abortions. Although it is desirable to reduce this type of sterility, its impact on fertility levels may be very significant in the future, especially in Africa.

(f) Usage of contraception

Any practice undertaken deliberately to reduce the risk of conception is classed as contraception, whether it be a centuries-old traditional method or a modern twentieth-century technique. In many societies some form of contraception has always been practised, indicating that couples have always been aware of the possibilities of limiting family size, no matter how successful the technique. However, from the 1960s onwards, modern methods of contraception, most notably the oral contraceptive pill, were improved and because of their relatively cheap cost and their reliability became widely used in the developed world. In the late 1960s and early 1970s modern contraceptive devices became available to developing countries and the dramatic decline in fertility since recorded in many of these countries has been attributed to this technology.

Table 4.1 shows the recent contraception prevalence rates and total fertility rates in thirty-two developing countries and eight developed countries. There are marked differences between the two groups in terms of fertility levels as well as in use of contraception. Among the more developed countries listed, contraception was used by well over 60% of all married women. The total fertility rate was below the replacement level of 2.1 births per woman in all the developed countries listed. Among the developing countries, contraception usage is highest in Latin America, with Costa Rica recording the highest usage of 66%, and a fertility level of 3.3. Lowest levels of contraception use are to be found in sub-Saharan Africa, with only Zimbabwe recording a usage rate of over 10%. Even Zimbabwe's contraception usage rate of 38% still resulted in a fertility rate of 6.5; only in Botswana and Lesotho are fertility rates lower than 6.

The variations in fertility among countries, between regions and socio-economic strata within countries, and among individual women, are due to the effects of one or more of the proximate determinants discussed above. Although it is impossible to measure the impact of all the proximate determinants, it is possible to estimate

118

Table 4.1   Gross National Product per capita, percentage of married women using contraception and fertility rates in 40 selected countries (Source: World Bank, 1989)

Rank	Country	GNP per capita $	% married women using contraception	Total fertility rate	Female literacy %
1	Nepal	160	15	5.9	12
2	Benin	310	6	6.5	16
3	Kenya	330	17	7.7	49
4	Pakistan	350	11	6.7	19
5	Nigeria	370	5	6.5	31
6	Sri Lanka	400	62	2.7	83
7	Mauritania	440	1	6.5	n.a.
8	Indonesia	450	48	3.5	65
9	Senegal	520	12	6.5	19
10	Bolivia	580	26	6.1	65
11	Philippines	590	44	3.9	85
12	Morocco	610	36	4.8	22
13	Egypt	680	32	4.8	30
14	Honduras	810	35	5.6	58
15	Thailand	850	65	2.8	88
16	El Salvador	860	48	4.9	69
17	Jamaica	940	52	2.9	100
18	Guatemala	950	23	5.8	47
19	Paraguay	990	49	4.6	85
20	Ecuador	1 040	44	4.3	80
21	Botswana	1 050	29	5.0	69
22	Tunisia	1 180	41	4.1	41
23	Colombia	1 240	63	3.2	88
24	Peru	1 470	46	4.1	78
25	Jordan	1 560	26	6.5	63
26	Costa Rica	1 610	66	3.3	93
27	Malaysia	1 810	51	3.8	66
28	Mexico	1 830	53	3.6	88
29	Panama	2 240	61	3.1	88
30	S. Korea	2 690	70	2.1	91
31	Trinidad & Tobago	4 210	54	2.8	95
32	Singapore	7 940	74	1.7	79
33	Australia	11 100	67	1.9	100
34	Belgium	11 480	81	1.6	100
35	Netherlands	11 860	72	1.6	100
36	W. Germany	14 400	78	1.4	100
37	Sweden	15 550	78	1.9	100
38	Japan	15 760	64	1.7	100
39	USA	18 530	68	1.9	100
40	Switzerland	21 330	70	1.6	100

the percentage increase in fertility that would occur if the fertility-inhibiting effect of each of the determinants was removed. This is shown in Figure 4.4, and demonstrates that the elimination of breastfeeding and postpartum abstinence would produce a 72% increase in fertility in Africa, whereas in Latin America, the elimination of contraception would result in a 54% increase in fertility. Figure 4.5 shows that globally the increased use of contraception is responsible for 90% of

Figure 4.4   Estimated percentage of increase in fertility associated with the removal of fertility-inhibiting effect of various proximate variables (Source: Bongaarts, Frank & Lesthaeghe, 1984)

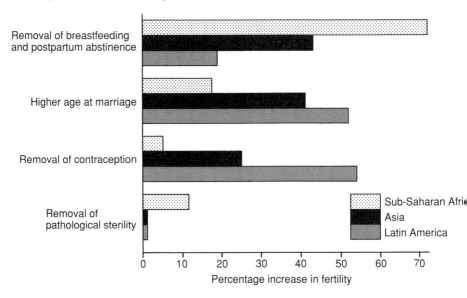

Figure 4.5   Estimated contribution of proximate determinants to fertility decline (Source: World Bank Development Report 1984. Copyright © 1984 by the International Bank for Reconstruction and Development/The World Bank. Reprinted by permission of Oxford University Press, Inc.)

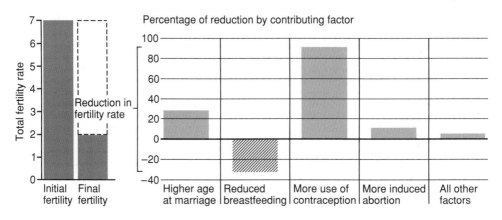

fertility reduction, while the increased age of women at marriage has contributed 25% to the decline. On the negative side, reduced duration of breastfeeding has slowed down fertility decline.

2. Socio-economic determinants

There are two main socio-economic factors that have a significant impact on fertility levels: i) the economic and social value of children, and ii) the economic and social status of women.

(a) The economic and social value of children

High population increase is often said to be detrimental to the economic development of many poorer countries. This is because it is blamed for suppressing GNP *per capita*, a common measure of economic development. But very often what appears to be detrimental at the national scale is totally rational at the household level. For instance, in 1976 J.C. Caldwell put forward the theory of *Wealth Flows* to explain both stable high fertility and the onset of sustained fertility decline at the household level. It is a theory which attempts to explain fertility trends by analysing the economic value of children to the parents. The theory suggests that in households where children make an economic contribution at an early age, through either wage employment, helping on the family farm or freeing adults (especially women) from domestic tasks such as collecting water and fuelwood, then fertility will be high. In this situation *wealth flows* from the child to the household, and therefore restricting fertility produces no economic gain to the household. But when education withdraws

Plate 4.2   Indian girls beat coconut husks, providing a small income for their families. In this case wealth is flowing from the child to the household, perhaps encouraging high fertility rates. (Photograph: G. O'Hare)

Plate 4.3   In most Third World societies girls are the porters of domestic water, as here in India. This makes them an important and necessary part of the household. (Photograph: G. O'Hare)

children from household production and imposes direct costs on the parents for school fees, uniforms and books, then *wealth flows* in the reverse direction, from the household to the child. In this instance the household will gain economically from restricting family size. In short, the theory states that as the importance of children to the domestic and formal sector labour force declines, and the costs of raising and educating children increase, then fertility will automatically decline.

The economic costs of children to the household can be divided into two. First the cost to the parents of goods and services that the child consumes during rearing, particularly food, shelter, clothing, medical care and education. Secondly the amount of time that parents put into caring for children, which can be translated into loss of income, especially that of the mother. The economic benefits of children include their direct contribution to the household economy as well as their value in providing security for their parents in old age. This latter consideration is very important in many developing countries where there are no social security provisions in the form of pensions for elderly people. It is less important in the developed countries where old-age pensions are provided.

Few parents explicitly make such cold economic calculations when deciding on family size. However, investigations do show that *wealth flows* are a consideration in many households. In the USA, for example, the cost of supporting a child to the age of eighteen, excluding any costs of higher education, is over $100 000, and half of all women using contraception are doing so because they feel they cannot afford a child. In contrast, in Bangladesh, boys produce more than they consume by the age of ten, and have repaid their parents' investment in them by the time they are fifteen years old. Likewise in Java, Indonesia, children are net income earners by the age of nine. In the Philippines nearly half the cost of rearing a child

122

Table 4.2   The benefits and costs of the economic, social and psychological values attached to children

	Benefits	Costs
Economic	Help with domestic chores. Financial contribution to household. Security in old age.	Cost of education. Cost of food, clothing, and shelter. Loss of parental wage earnings.
Social	Companionship, love, happiness. Marital bonds strengthened. Continuation of family name.	Mental strains. Overcrowding of family residence.
Psychological	Fulfilment. Living through children. Incentive to succeed.	Parents feeling tied down. Emotional strain. Disciplinary problems.

is offset by receipts from child earnings, work at home and old age support. These differences are caused by the relative economic value of children in different societies. It is therefore economically rational for many families in the Third World, especially those in rural areas that are heavily reliant on family labour, to maintain high fertility levels, even if on the national scale this is undesirable.

Unrealistically, the theory of *wealth flows* takes into account only the economic costs and benefits of children. However, the social and psychological values attached to children which are listed in Table 4.2 must also be considered. These may include the companionship, love, happiness and fun of having children. Children may also strengthen marital bonds as well as providing psychological fulfilment to the parents. But there may also be costs, such as emotional stress and marital strain. Figure 4.6 shows the variety of values and drawbacks of children reported by mothers in the Philippines, South Korea and the USA. The economic contribution of children is considered more important in the Philippines than in the other two countries, perhaps explaining the higher fertility rate there. Of the three, fertility is lowest in the USA, which may in turn reflect the restrictions that children are perceived to impose upon parents. However, 73% of US mothers taking part in the survey said that the social and psychological value of children was their main reason for having them; only 4% cited economic support as a reason. It would appear, therefore, that the perceived and actual values attached to children by parents can have a direct impact on fertility trends.

(b) The economic and social status of women

Any discussion concerning the status of women involves the consideration of many aspects of society. Societies where women have legal and political equality with men, as well as having the same social and economic opportunities as men, are rare, even in the developed world. Measuring the status of women within any

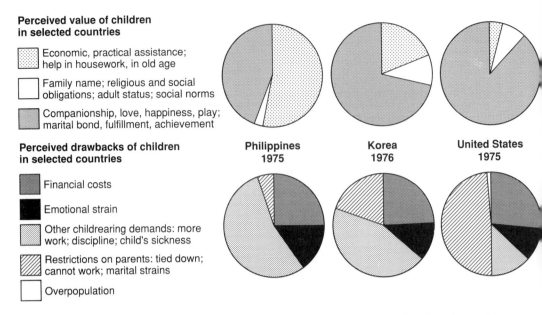

Perceived value of children in selected countries

▪ Economic, practical assistance; help in housework, in old age

▫ Family name; religious and social obligations; adult status; social norms

▪ Companionship, love, happiness, play; marital bond, fulfillment, achievement

Perceived drawbacks of children in selected countries

▪ Financial costs

▪ Emotional strain

▪ Other childrearing demands: more work; discipline; child's sickness

▨ Restrictions on parents: tied down; cannot work; marital strains

▫ Overpopulation

Philippines 1975   Korea 1976   United States 1975

Figure 4.6   Perceived values and drawbacks of children by parents in selected countries (Source: World Bank Development Report, 1984)

society is difficult, but two indicators have been given prominence as they indirectly affect other factors that are less easy to quantify. The first measure is the level of female education, the second is the integration of women into the formal sector of the economy.

i) *Female education.* This factor affects fertility indirectly by improving child survival rates. Female education is important if campaigns such as those to promote the advantages of breastfeeding and warn of the dangers of bottle-feeding are to be successful. Education is also important for the spread of knowledge concerning oral rehydration therapy and the benefits of immunisation programmes, as well as the acceptance of contraceptive advice. A mother who is literate has more opportunity to learn about new ideas and more confidence to put them into practice. For the majority of children, the most important healthcare worker is the mother. It is not surprising, therefore, to find a large body of data establishing that the level of a mother's education is a key determinant of her offspring's health.

Work done in Indonesia and Pakistan shows that infant mortality rates among children whose mothers have had four or more years of education was 50% lower than among children whose mothers were illiterate. In Latin America, studies have shown that the influence of female education is a stronger variable than household income in explaining child survival rates. One researcher has even gone as far as saying that 86% of the decline in Kenya's infant mortality rate over the last twenty years can be explained by the rise in female education. Whatever the actual figures, the evidence points conclusively to the fact that female education can have a direct impact on child survival rates. UNICEF claim that investing in a minimum of four

Plate 4.4   There is a strong correlation between female education, infant mortality and fertility. This photograph shows girls in school in Britain at the turn of the century, enjoying a health education lesson on dental hygiene. Each girl is holding a tooth brush. The caption on the blackboard reads: 'Spare the brush and spoil the teeth.' (Photograph: The Mansell Collection)

years schooling for every girl is one of the most cost-effective investments any country can make in its own future. Despite this, registration rates of girls in primary school vary. Rates of less than fifty girls per hundred boys registered at primary school are recorded in a number of developing countries including Yemen (24), Chad (39) and Nepal (41). In other countries, such as the UK, all girls must attend school to the age of sixteen.

The influence of female education on child survival rates also has an indirect impact on birth rates, as declines in infant mortality usually precede decreases in the fertility rate. Child survival tends to reduce birth rates in three separate ways. First, child survival means that a mother continues to breastfeed, which provides her with a natural contraceptive. In the Indian state of Kerala the death of a child in its first month of life reduces the average interval between births from three years to less than two. Secondly, child survival means that parents can more confidently plan the number of children they want, rather than having 'extra' children to compensate for those who may die. If parents are assured that their children will survive to adulthood, research shows they are more likely to use an effective method of family planning. Thirdly, child survival results in a change in mentality of parents, from a sense of 'destiny' to that of control over their own lives. Female education can therefore ultimately affect birth rates by reducing infant mortality.

125

An increase in child survival rates results in a slowing down of the rate of population growth. However, female employment outside the family also contributes to this decline.

ii) *Female participation in the formal economy.* When women have limited access to paid employment and education, and their primary task is unpaid family labour, fertility rates are high. A recent study comparing 79 Third World countries in 1970 and 1980 shows strong correlations between declining fertility rates and rising educational attainment and increased employment opportunities for women. Career structures and working hours in most countries assume that the worker has no domestic responsibilities. This explains why women, who make up half of the world's adult population, account for only a third of the official, cash-earning labour force. Domestic duties, especially concerned with child-care, prevent many women from working full time. The implications for fertility are obvious.

Many women who want to participate fully and equitably in the formal labour market see children as a disadvantage. The economic costs of having children, in terms of lost earnings, can be high for women, especially in societies where provisions are not made to accommodate mothers into the work force. For example, it was estimated in 1985 that the cost to the average UK mother of bringing up two children was $88 200 in lost earnings. Because of the inflexibility of formal employment many women have to take part-time positions. In the UK, for example, 41% of employed women and 2% of men are working part-time, and one in twenty-five women teachers and one in twelve female nurses abandons her career because of family commitments and now works part-time in a cleaning or catering job. This is a dreadful waste of a nation's resources.

The socio-economic status of women has a marked impact on fertility levels. This is an under-researched topic but one which is increasingly coming to the attention of the population geographer. Despite a dearth of data it is one variable that must be taken into account when considering fertility trends and patterns.

3. Institutional policies concerning population

Institutional policies concerning population growth rates can and often do affect fertility by manipulating socio-economic determinants which in turn affect the proximate determinants, a relationship shown in Figure 4.7. There are two major institutions that influence the fertility decisions of parents: government policies; and religious philosophy.

(a) Government policies

Governments can affect fertility rates through policies providing family planning programmes, health care facilities and financial incentives. Such policies reflect any government's political position on desired family size and population growth rates. These policies can have profound impacts on fertility trends by manipulating proximate determinants through socio-economic variables. Because government policies are so influential in determining fertility patterns they will be dealt with

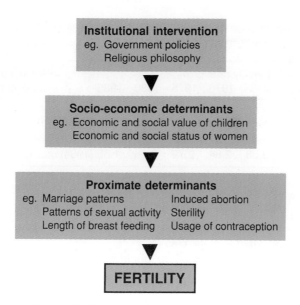

Figure 4.7   Factors affecting fertility patterns

more fully in Chapter 6. Both proximate and socio-economic determinants of fertility can and often are influenced by government policies.

(b) Religious philosophy

Most of the world's main religions (Buddhism, Christianity, Hinduism, Islam, Judaism) favour fertility and encourage parents to have large families. Within a religion, though, there may be differences, as demonstrated by the attitudes towards contraception by Roman Catholics and Protestants within the Christian faith. The example of much higher fertility levels amongst Catholic French-speaking Canadians over that of English-speaking Protestant Canadians is often quoted. However, this differential can also be explained by political factors. French-speaking Canadians who predominantly settled in Quebec felt politically threatened by a large influx of Protestant English-speaking migrants during the first half of this century. This political threat combined with differing religious beliefs may well account for the differential fertility. At the present time the difference between the fertility levels of the two groups is narrowing.

Fertility level differences between Roman Catholic and Protestant populations have been narrowing since 1965, and some demographers now claim that there will be little difference between the two by the end of the century. Table 4.3 shows the fertility rates of Europe's three staunchest Roman Catholic populations, Eire, Italy and Spain, over the period 1965-1985. In all three countries fertility rates have declined, and although fertility in Eire is still higher than in other European countries the decline in fertility of women aged 20-24 during the decade 1976-1986 was twice the equivalent fall in the UK. The decline in fertility rates in the Roman

Table 4.3   Fertility rates and proportion of illegitimate births in four European countries, 1965–1985 (Source: UK Birth Statistics, 1987)

	Fertility rate					% illegitimate births of total births
	1965	1970	1975	1980	1985	
UK	2.86	2.44	1.81	1.89	1.80	21
Italy	2.67	2.42	2.21	1.69	1.46 (1984)	5
Eire	4.03	3.87	3.40	3.23	2.49	10
Spain	3.08	2.84	2.79	2.16	1.65 (1984)	4

Catholic countries of Europe has been so rapid that in 1985 fertility rates in Italy and Spain were lower than that of the UK. The social power of the Catholic religion is, however, still noticeable by the low number of illegitimate births in these countries compared with the UK.

Although Islam is not opposed to population planning policies, religious conservatism often results in it not being given a high priority. This means that some of the richest countries in the world, which also happen to be Islamic, such as United Arab Emirates with a GNP per capita of $14 680 in 1986 and Kuwait with a GNP per capita of $13 890 (compared with a UK GNP per capita in 1986 of $8870) have high fertility rates of 5.7 and 4.8 respectively, compared with the UK fertility rate of 1.8. Demographically, the Islamic populations of the world stand out in contrast to other nations of similar economic development, having low death rates but high birth rates (see Chapter 2). The only explanation for their unique demographic characteristics is that of religious philosophy.

Islam may well account for the high fertility rates of Bangladeshi and Pakistani mothers resident in the UK, compared with other ethnic groups. In 1986 the fertility rate of mothers born in Bangladesh and Pakistan was 5.6, compared with 1.8 for those mothers born in the Caribbean, 2.0 for those born in East Africa, 2.8 for those born in the rest of Africa and 1.7 for those born in the UK. The importance of religious philosophy in affecting fertility levels must not be underestimated, particularly when combined with political control, as has occurred in many states.

ASSIGNMENTS

1. (a) What is meant by the term 'proximate determinant' of fertility?
   (b) Study Figures 4.4 and 4.5 and comment on the importance of the various proximate determinants on fertility levels.
2. (a) Summarise the theory of wealth flows.
   (b) With reference to Figure 4.6, assess the importance of wealth flows to families in the Third World.
3. (a) Using the data in Table 4.1, plot scattergraphs of female literacy with
      i) total fertility rate, and ii) percentage of married women using contraception.
   (b) Describe the relationships shown on the graphs.
   (c) With reference to your results discuss the relationship between female literacy and fertility.

4. *(a) List the type of institutional policies that could affect fertility.*
   (b) Using Figure 4.7 as a framework, explain how these policies influence
       fertility patterns.

C. Case Studies

1. Infertility in sub-Saharan Africa

In 1985 sub-Saharan Africa had approximately 432 million people living in thirty-seven countries. Approximately half the population lived in the largest five countries: Nigeria (95 million), Ethiopia (43 million), Zaire (30 million), Tanzania (22 million) and Sudan (21.5 million). The share of the world's population living in this region increased from 6.2% in 1950 to 8.9% in 1985.

The demographic characteristics of sub-Saharan Africa are unique, because its birth rates and death rates are higher than any other region in the world. This has resulted in the highest regional population growth rate (2.9%) in the world. At the same time Africa has a pattern of infertility quite different from other regions of the world. The results of a survey undertaken by the World Health Organisation, summarised in Table 4.4, illustrate this difference. The Table shows that African women experience infertility at a much earlier age than women elsewhere. Forty-two per cent of the women investigated were infertile by the age of twenty-four, compared with an average of 23% in other regions. As a result the proportion of African women becoming infertile in the other age groups is lower than that experienced in other regions. Infertility in men in all regions occurs at a later age than for women, the majority occurring in the 25-34 age group.

Table 4.4   Patterns of global infertility

	% of infertile couples				
	Developed countries	Africa	Asia	Latin America	East Mediterranean
Age of woman					
under 24	25	42	22	24	24
25–34	68	52	70	65	69
over 35	7	6	8	11	7
Age of man					
under 24	10	5	4	11	2
25–34	72	60	70	62	53
over 35	18	35	26	27	45
Type of infertility					
Primary	71	48	77	60	84
Secondary	29	52	23	40	16

Table 4.4 shows that Africa is also different from other parts of the world in the proportion of couples unable to have any children, known as *primary sterility*, as compared to those couples experiencing sterility after the birth of one or more children, technically labelled *secondary sterility*. Of the couples investigated in Africa only 48% were suffering primary infertility, compared with an average of 73% in the rest of the world. Secondary infertility was suffered by 52% of couples, twice the figure reported in other regions. This figure for secondary infertility in Africa indicates a high level of pathological sterility, a view that was confirmed by the WHO survey. Over 85% of sterility in African women is caused by infection, particularly sexually transmitted diseases such as gonorrhoea and infections which result from unhygienic abortion practices. This would indicate a correspondingly high prevalence of sexually transmitted diseases amongst African men.

The single major cause of infertility in sub-Saharan Africa is gonorrhoea. This sexually transmitted disease is not life-threatening, and has been given little weight as a health problem in Africa. However, gonorrhoea rates reported by thirteen African countries to WHO between 1967 and 1973 showed an inverse relationship with their crude birth rates. Penicillin campaigns in the 1950s targeted at sexually transmitted diseases such as *yaws* and *pinta* (*syphilis*-type diseases), resulted in increased fertility in Cameroon, Burkina Faso, Zaire and Zambia. Since then these diseases have been largely ignored by governments and health campaigns. Only two sub-Saharan African countries mentioned sexually transmitted diseases in their reports to WHO concerning their health situation in the 1970s, and Cameroon was the only country to cite them as a major communicable disease problem. Sexually transmitted diseases appear to be a source of embarrassment to African governments.

Primary infertility, as indicated by childlessness, is shown on Figure 4.8. This map shows that infertility is present in almost all areas, but the level of infertility varies markedly, even between neighbouring small areas. Sterility is negligible in Burundi, most of Kenya, Southern Sudan and in Ankole, Uganda. But in central Africa, including Northern Zaire, Gabon, Central African Republic, Congo and Cameroon, very high levels of sterility occur. This map of infertility corresponds not only with levels of fertility, but also with patterns of ethnicity. This suggests that ethnic distribution is a significant aspect of African infertility. Because gonorrhoea is sexually transmitted, the variability of infertility by ethnic distribution suggests that differences in ethnic patterns of sexual behaviour play an important part in determining levels of infertility in Africa. Studies show that in societies where sexual mobility, such as premarital sex and illegitimacy, divorce and remarriage, polygamy, extramarital sex and prostitution, are acceptable, infertility levels are high.

A reduction in current levels of infertility in Africa would be a powerful source of population growth and most certainly would contribute to an increase in the already high fertility rates of the region. It is estimated that infertility accounts for 60% of the variation in total fertility between sub-Saharan African countries, and if pathological infertility was reduced to levels accepted as normal in developed countries, then total fertility would increase by 15%. Although it is recognised that infertility is a serious health problem in Africa, in the late 1980s concern has shifted from sexually transmitted, but curable diseases, such as gonorrhoea, to the

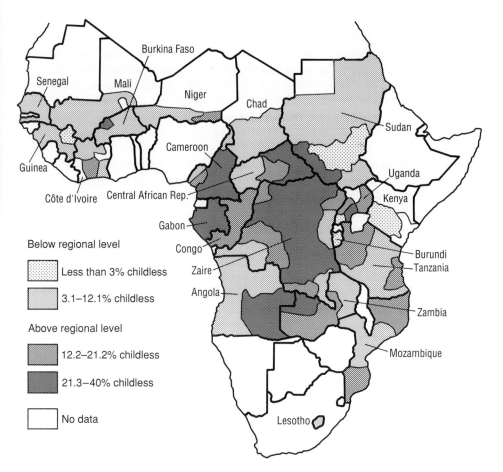

Figure 4.8   Levels in childlessness among women aged 45–49 years in 21 sub-Saharan African countries (Source: Frank, 1983)

spread of Acquired Immune-Deficiency Syndrome (AIDS). Although AIDS does not produce infertility, its impact on the demography of Africa may be more devastating.

Africa is the part of world most severely affected by the AIDS pandemic. WHO estimates that more than two million Africans may be infected with the virus, out of a possible five to ten million cases worldwide. By 1995 WHO predicts that up to 75 million people in Africa will be dead or dying from the disease. The AIDS epidemic is worse in Central, Eastern and Southern Africa, and is spreading rapidly in areas of labour migration. The most rapid increases appear to be occurring along the south-eastern migrant workers' route, linking Somalia, Kenya, Uganda, Rwanda, Burundi, Zaire, Zambia, Zimbabwe, Mozambique and South Africa.

The AIDS epidemic in Africa is different from that in Europe and USA, in that half the cases are women, compared with less than 10% in the Western world. In a hospital in Kampala, Uganda, 18% of female blood donors were found to be infected, compared with 14% of male donors. As AIDS in Africa is spread predominantly by heterosexual contact, prostitution is believed to be a major route by which the disease is spread. In one African country a sample of prostitutes undertaken in 1980-81 revealed that 4% of the women were HIV positive, but by 1985-6 a similar survey showed that 59% of the prostitutes were infected with the AIDS virus. These figures show how rapidly the virus can spread through a population. The age group most at risk of infection in Africa is the 16-29 age group, where 10% of women aged 16-19 are already infected as compared to 4% of men.

The nature and extent of the AIDS epidemic in Africa has serious implications for the future demography of the continent, as well as endangering its future economic development. As large numbers of economically active adults die prematurely, fertility rates and economic productivity will decline. AIDS infection in African children is already a serious problem. In some areas 2-10% of pregnant women are infected with the virus and half of the children born to these mothers may be infected with the virus from birth. This epidemic threatens to undermine the health gains and declines in mortality experienced by all African countries since 1945, at the same time reducing fertility. The implication is that the AIDS epidemic in Africa may transform the demography of the continent by the end of the century and thus make the issue of high fertility rates irrelevant.

2. Married women, fertility and labour force participation in the USA

In virtually every industrial country the proportion of married women in paid employment has risen dramatically since 1945. In general the more developed the country and the longer it has been industrialised, the higher the proportion of married women in the labour force. The exceptions are the socialist countries of Europe where the proportion is high regardless of the degree of development and is primarily a result of a small labour force and the egalitarian philosophy of socialism. In Bulgaria, for example, 83.8% of married women in 1975 were in the labour force. In the USA, as Table 4.5 shows, only 4.6% of married women were in the labour force in 1890, but by 1950 the figure had risen to 23.8%. This upward trend continued until in 1970 the figure was 40.8% and by 1986 59% of all married women went out to work. Other industrial countries have shown a similar trend with the percentage of married women in the work force varying from 47.8% in France to 62.9% in Sweden.

Although women's labour is more important to the USA economy now than at any other time in history, there is a distinct difference in the participation rate of married women in the work force based on colour. A greater proportion of black married women go out to work than white married women. Of married women with children, 74% of black mothers go out to work, compared with 61% of white mothers. This perhaps reflects the lower income levels of black families. Thirty-four per cent of black families earned less than $10 000pa in 1986, compared with 12% of white families. At the other end of the spectrum only 5.8% of black

Plate 4.5   In 1986, 59% of all married women in the USA belonged to the labour force. Many have children to care for and as a result may only be able to take part-time positions. These hospital workers in New York, the majority of whom are women (many part-time), are attending a trade union meeting to discuss better wages and conditions of service. (Photograph: Gina Glover/Photo Co-op)

Table 4.5   Percentage of married women in the labour force, Crude birth rate, fertility rate and divorce rate in USA, 1890–1985 (Source: USA Abstract of Statistics, 1987)

	% of married women in labour force	CBR per 1000	Fertility rate per woman	Divorces per 1000 population
1890	4.6	–	–	–
1900	5.6	–	–	–
1910	10.7	30.1	–	0.9
1920	9.0	27.7	–	1.6
1930	11.7	21.3	–	1.6
1940	14.7	19.4	2.7	2.0
1950	23.8	23.9	3.3	2.6
1955	27.7	24.9	3.7	2.3
1960	30.5	23.8	3.5	2.2
1965	34.7	19.6	2.9	2.5
1970	40.8	18.2	2.5	3.5
1975	44.4	14.6	1.8	4.8
1980	50.1	15.9	1.8	5.2
1985	55.0	15.7	1.8	5.0

– data not available

families earned over $50 000pa, compared with 17% of white families. The lowest median income in 1986 was earned by Puerto Rican families ($12 371), followed by black families ($15 432), Mexican families ($19 184) and topped by white families ($27 686). A desire to retain or advance one's own and one's children's status in a rapidly evolving society is obviously one important reason why many mothers go out to work. The fact that 61% of mothers with children under the age of 18 are economically productive as opposed to 48% of married women with no children, implies that the *flow of wealth* from parents to children in the USA, encourages or may even necessitate that mothers go out to work.

There is, however, another factor that must be considered, that of marital instability, manifested by separations and divorce. The divorce rate in the USA has increased from 0.9 per 1000 population in 1910 to 5.0 per 1000 in 1985 (see Table 4.5). As divorce rates have increased many women have chosen to participate in the labour force as an insurance against the financial hardship and insecurity associated with divorce. In 1985, for example, 9.6% of households were female single parent units as compared to 1.4% male single parents units. These figures disguise large ethnic differences which are shown in Table 4.6. The large number of Puerto Rican and black single parent families stands out. The financial insecurity associated with separation or divorce perhaps explains the very high labour force participation rates of these groups of women shown in Table 4.7. In total, 62% of separated women work and 77% of divorced women work, a much higher proportion than married women. The risk of divorce may encourage low fertility rates, because unstable unions weaken the long and dedicated commitment required for child

Table 4.6   Percentage of female and male single parent families by ethnic group in USA, 1985 (Source: USA Abstract of Statistics, 1987)

	Puerto Rican	Black	Mexican	White	National average
Female single-parent families	34.3%	28.7%	13.4%	7.2%	9.6%
Male single-parent families	2.6%	1.9%	1.5%	1.4%	1.4%

Table 4.7   Proportions of married, separated and divorced women, with children of various ages, who are in the US labour force (Source: USA Abstract of Statistics, 1987)

	No children under 18 years old	With children under 6 years old	With children between 6–17 years old
Married women	48%	54%	68%
Separated women	60%	57%	70%
Divorced women	72%	74%	85%

care. A woman can bring up a child on her own in most developed societies, often with government financial support, but she is unlikely to choose to have a large number of children. This is explained by the fact that she usually has to go out to work to support herself and her children and at the same time does not have a partner to share the chores and worries of domestic production and childcare.

The economic need and desire of many married women to join the US work force, whether they are mothers or not, may well be a major factor in explaining the 50% reduction of the CBR over the period 1910-1985 (shown in Table 4.5). The US fertility rate halved between 1950-1985, and is now below replacement level.

It is clear that married women in the developed world are returning to economic production. In some societies they are being actively encouraged to do so, due to gloomy forecasts of impending labour shortages. But unless society recognises that women are social reproducers as well as economic producers and provision is made for the former, then fertility rates in these industrialised countries will remain below replacement level and will exacerbate predicted labour shortages. It is a problem that many Western nations are going to have to come to terms with in the next decade or so. It is very unlikely that women will give up their new-found economic freedom and independence to become reproducers of the labour force, as was the case at the beginning of this century.

ASSIGNMENTS

1. *(a) How does infertility in Africa differ from other global regions?*
   (b) What appears to be the major cause of infertility in this region?
   (c) What impact on fertility rates might result from the reduction of infertility in Africa?
   (d) Discuss the likely demographic impact of the AIDS epidemic in Africa.
2. *(a) Graph the data presented in Table 4.5.*
   (b) Describe the trends.
   (c) What relationships can be drawn from this data?
   (d) Look at Table 4.7. Discuss the role of marital instability in encouraging women to enter the US labour force.
   (e) What may be the potential impact on fertility?

Key Ideas

Introduction

1. Fertility, unlike mortality, depends on individual decisions.
2. Fertility can be measured in a number of ways: crude birth rates, total fertility rate and total fertility rate per woman.

A. Geography of fertility

1. The highest global birth rates are to be found in Africa, and the lowest in Europe.

2. Since 1965 there have been significant decreases in CBRs in many parts of the world. Only in Africa have CBRs not declined.

B. Factors affecting fertility

1. There are three inter-connected factors that affect fertility rates: proximate determinants; socio-economic factors; and institutional intervention.
2. Proximate determinants are the behavioural and biological factors that directly affect fertility. They include: marriage patterns; patterns of sexual activity; duration of breastfeeding; the number of induced abortions; levels of sterility; and the proportion of couples using contraception.
3. There are two socio-economic factors that have a significant impact on fertility levels: the economic and social value of children; and the economic and social status of women.
4. In societies where female education rates are high and female participation rates in the formal economy are important, fertility rates tend to be low.
5. Institutional policies often affect fertility by manipulating socio-economic determinants. The major institutions that can affect fertility decisions are government policy and religious philosophy.

C. Case Studies

1. Although CBRs in sub-Saharan Africa are the highest in the world, the region also suffers a pattern of infertility quite different from other parts of the globe.
2. The major cause of sterility in sub-Saharan Africa is sexually transmitted infection. African women experience infertility at a much younger age than women elsewhere.
3. In virtually all western countries, including the USA, the proportion of married women in paid employment has increased since 1945.
4. The participation of women in the US economy is considered a major factor in explaining the 50% reduction in the US birth rate between 1910 and 1985.

Additional Activities

1. Although crude birth rates globally are declining, the world's population will continue to increase. Explain why this is the case.
2. Discuss how the Wealth Flows Theory may explain fertility decline as described by the Demographic Transition Model in Chapter 2.
3. Examine the impact on the fertility levels of female status within society. Use material from this chapter as well as Chapter 2 to support your arguments. Refer also to Table 4.8 below.

Table 4.8 Relationship between the total fertility rate and female status in 79 Third World countries, 1980 (Source: 'World Resources', International Institute for Environment and Development, 1987)

Number of countries	Total fertility rate	Women's share of paid employment %	Women's literacy rate %	Women's elementary school completion rate %	Women's average age at marriage
9	over 7.0	11	34	17	20
35	6.1–7.0	17	23	10	19
10	5.1–6.0	25	54	26	21
25	5 or less	30	77	54	22

5 Migration as a Component of Population Change

Introduction

Together with fertility and mortality, migration forms a third fundamental element in determining population growth and structure. Indeed, migration is such an important component of population change that geographers have devoted more attention to the study of migration than to any other branch of population geography. Past human migration has played a major role in shaping the cultural map of the world, and is the demographic basis of societies such as the USA, Canada and Australia. Between 1800 and 1950, for instance, 60 million Europeans migrated overseas, 40 million of whom settled in the USA. Present and future migrations may be equally important, especially in Europe, where many populations are experiencing low birth and death rates.

Migration is not easy to define, but usually involves the permanent or semi-permanent change in residence of an individual. Migration begins in an area of *origin* and is completed at an area of *destination* and may involve a stay of one year or more. When migrants cross an international frontier they are termed either *emigrants* if they are leaving or *immigrants* if they are entering a country. Migrants who move within a country are referred to as *out-migrants* or *in-migrants*. If large numbers of migrants are involved, the movement is referred to as a *migration stream or flow*. Migration should not be confused with circulation, which refers to short-term repetitive or cyclical movements such as shopping trips, commuting and holidays. Both circulation and migration are embraced by the general term *mobility*.

There are four aspects of migration that the population geographer should consider. First, the various types of migration need to be distinguished and classified. Secondly, it is necessary to identify the factors that influence migration. Thirdly, appropriate theories must be developed to explain population movements. Fourthly, consideration should be given to the impact of migration on both areas of origin and destination.

A. Types of Migration

Numerous attempts have been made to classify the movements of people, using different criteria. The criteria most commonly used are distance, time and area of origin.

138

1. Distance

Distance is the criteria most commonly used to distinguish migrants. The difference between internal and international migration is stressed. This classification ignores the cultural or social distance travelled by a migrant. For example, the cultural distance travelled by a Dutch emigrant into Switzerland, might be far lower than an Indian out-migrant moving from a village to Calcutta. Nevertheless this classification is the one most favoured by population geographers.

2. Time

Time is used to distinguish between temporary and permanent migration. Much labour migration, for example, is temporary in nature, in that the migrant moves to find work and may be away for a number of years. Other migrants may decide to move permanently, as with many people moving from rural to urban areas. However, the use of time as a criterion has its problems, as many temporary migrants may in fact become permanent migrants, and many permanent migrants decide to move back to their area of origin. However, in combination with other criteria, this categorisation may be useful.

3. Origin

A common form of classifying migration in geographical literature is to use the area of origin. This usually means defining the migrant's area of origin as either rural or urban. Though this has proved to be a useful classification, the difference between rural and urban in many developed countries is becoming less distinguishable.

B. Factors affecting Migration

A number of factors affect migration. These include economic, social and ecological considerations, which are all in turn affected by individual perceptions and behaviour (see Figure 5.1). Very rarely do these factors operate in isolation, and it is often difficult to distinguish between factors, for example economic and ecological factors may act together, as may economic and social factors. These factors, in whatever combination, act in such a way to *push* and *pull* migrants. For example, economic factors such as unemployment, may *push* a migrant to seek employment elsewhere, but the destination that is chosen may be determined by social factors, in other words the migrant may be *pulled* to a location by its recreational possibilities, such as a golf course, or the nearness of friends and relatives.

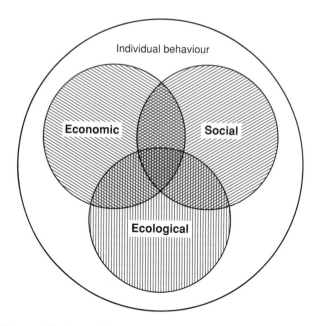

Figure 5.1   Factors affecting decisions to migrate

1. Economic factors

Economic factors are often regarded as the major motivation for migration. The principal economic factor is the search for employment (or labour), accompanied by the exploitation of natural resources such as minerals and the availability of good communication networks, for instance navigable waterways.

The growth of economically related migration is often regarded as indicative of the spread of world capitalism, which began in the late seventeenth century. The most notorious manifestation of movement caused purely by economic factors was the forced transfer of slaves from Africa to the Caribbean and American plantations in the seventeenth and eighteenth centuries. It is estimated that over ten million people were forcibly displaced from Africa, many of whom died before they reached their destination. Slavery was abolished in British colonies in 1830, and other countries followed (e.g. the USA in 1863). However, organisations such as Amnesty International claim that slavery still exists in spite of international agreements. What is certain is that the movement of people for economic reasons continues, both nationally and internationally.

In Western Europe it is estimated that there are over 15 million migrants and their families who came to meet the growing demand for labour in post war Europe. This labour shortage was caused by war losses and low birth rates, combined with improved working conditions such as longer holidays and shorter working weeks. At the same time, there was a proliferation of skilled jobs, so that indigenous workers became increasingly reluctant to take unskilled positions, such as building

Plate 5.1 It is estimated that over 10 million people were forcibly removed from Africa during the seventeenth and eighteenth centuries to work as slaves on the plantations in America and the Caribbean. They were worked very hard, often in inhumane conditions. This etching shows slaves working in a sugar plantation. Note the overseer with his whip. (Photograph: Mary Evans Picture Library)

labourers and bus conductors. As a result of publicity campaigns and government incentives, labour migrants came to Europe to fill the labour shortage, and principally filled the low status, unskilled or semi-skilled vacancies shunned by the indigenous population.

Many of the migrants moving into Western Europe in the post war period came from the Mediterranean countries of Greece, Turkey, Spain, Portugal, Italy and Yugoslavia. Others migrated from ex-colonial territories, for example, many migrants came to France from North Africa and the former French colonies in West Africa. Migration to the UK from the former British possessions of India, Pakistan and the Caribbean have been significant, as has been the migration into the Netherlands of nationals of the former Dutch colonies of the Antilles, Surinam and Indonesia.

Figure 5.2 shows the main areas of origin and destination of migration into Western Europe since 1945. However, the actual numbers of migrants in Europe are difficult to determine. This is due not only to illegal migration, but also to the fact that surveys and many censuses classify people as migrants only if they possess foreign passports. Many migrants from ex-colonies do in fact have European passports and are therefore excluded from official figures. The official number of labour migrants in Western Europe is therefore undoubtedly an underestimate. Despite these problems it is possible to use official statistics. In Switzerland the government estimates that there are over one million foreigners. These comprise 17% of the total population and over 25% of the labour force. France, the former

Plate 5.2   In the 1950s and 1960s thousands of migrants from the West Indies arrived in the UK to take up jobs. This picture, taken in 1962, shows some of these immigrants landing at Southampton to begin a new life. (Photograph: Popperfoto)

territory of West Germany and the UK each have about four million migrants, making up 5-10% of total population. The Netherlands, Belgium and Sweden, have smaller, but nevertheless substantial, foreign populations.

In Western Europe the trend has been for permanent labour migration, which includes the families of migrant workers joining them after a short time period. Many families have settled and integrated themselves with the host population. This is not necessarily the case in other areas where large transfers of labour take place.

South Africa is renowned for its reliance on migrant labour for the exploitation of its natural resources. Labour migration has been part of the Southern African scene for over a hundred years. It involves men from traditional subsistence farming areas being recruited to work on a temporary contractual basis in the modern economic sector of South Africa. Traditionally this type of migration was associated with the gold and diamond mines, but has now spread to almost every sector of the South African economy. In 1983 there were 1.8 million contractual migrants in South Africa. Of these 1.4 million came from the South African *Homelands* (areas designated by the South African government as independent states). The rest came from the nearby states of Mozambique, Malawi and Botswana. Labour is recruited by agencies, on long term contracts. The men are not allowed to bring their families with them and are often housed in squalid dormitory style accommodation. Labourers are allowed to return home to their families only when their contracts expire,

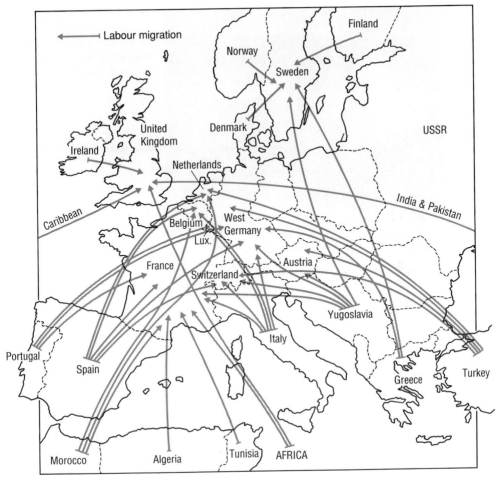

Figure 5.2   Origin and destination of labour migration into Western Europe (Source: Power, 1984)

usually every twelve months. This leaves many rural families in Southern Africa headed by women for long periods of time. It also results in labour shortages in many areas, forcing families to concentrate on subsistence cultivation rather than cash cropping. However, there may be some cash benefits, in that many migrants do send money back to their families.

Selectivity of labour migration is not restricted to Southern Africa. More recently, contractual male labour migration has surfaced in the six Gulf states of Bahrain, Kuwait, Oman, Qatar, Saudi Arabia and United Arab Emirates. In 1970 fewer than a million migrants worked in the Gulf states, but by 1980 this had rocketed to over six million and represented over 66% of the total labour force. This migration was triggered by an acute labour shortage and the oil price explosion of 1973-4, which enabled the Gulf states to buy in labour in large quantities and to embark on large construction programmes. Of the labour migrants working in the Gulf in 1980 two

Plate 5.3 The gold and diamond mines of South Africa have relied on black migrant labour for the last hundred years. Here at the Williamson Diamond Mine, black miners work on the rock face, 60 metres below the surface.
(Photograph: Popperfoto)

million were Arabs, 3.75 million were from Asia and the rest were from Africa, the Americas and Europe. Between 1981 and 1983 there were signs of recession in the Gulf as a result of a drop in oil prices and the Iran-Iraq War. Many migrants returned home, while those who stayed had to accept reductions in wages and conditions of service. Despite this, the demand for labour stayed high, as shown by the number of labour migrants working in the region at the start of the Gulf Crisis in the summer of 1990. It is estimated that three million foreign workers left Iraq and Kuwait between August and December 1990. The majority of these came from South Asia, Egypt and the Philippines, while Somalia, Sudan and Vietnam contributed sizeable numbers. Increasingly, labour migration can be seen as an international transfer of resources, similar to that of technology and capital.

2. Social factors

Social factors which may influence migration include social oppression, political control and the availability of housing, health care and education facilities. The most extreme example of migration caused by social factors is that of refugees. Refugees are defined by the United Nations High Commission for Refugees as: *'...persons who owing to well-founded fear of persecution for reasons of race, religion, nationality or political opinions, are outside their country of origin and cannot, or owing to such fear, do not wish to avail themselves of the protection of that country.'*

In the 1940s the major world refugee problem was in Europe, where over 25 million people were displaced by the war and subsequent changes in political

144

Plate 5.4   Escaping from political upheaval in Kampuchea, many people have fled to neighbouring countries for sanctuary. Here Kampuchean refugees live in an official camp in Thailand, waiting for conditions to change in their homeland. In 1985 there were over 200 000 refugees in Thailand. (Photograph: Ron Giling/Panos Pictures)

alignments and national boundaries. Today the greatest concentrations of refugees are in the Third World. In 1989 the official world refugee population was 14.5 million. Of these, 60% was made up of two single groups, six million Afghan refugees living in Iran and Pakistan, and 2.3 million Palestinians living in Jordan, Syria, Lebanon and the Israeli-occupied Gaza Strip and West Bank. Figure 5.3 shows the areas of origin and destination of official refugees and the numbers involved. Not included in the official figures are those many thousands of people who have independently left their homes, but have stayed within the boundaries of their own country.

Most refugees and those countries which initially accept them are in the developing world whose economies are least able to support large influxes of people. However, countries of final resettlement are most often in the West, including the USA which has taken 1.2 million refugees since 1975, Europe (0.5 million), Canada (0.2 million), and Australia (0.16 million). Nevertheless, in the late 1980s, perhaps due to economic recession and high unemployment rates, asylum-seekers were increasingly being designated as economic refugees by the West rather than political refugees. Thus for example in Hong Kong many Vietnamese *boat people* seeking political asylum have been repatriated to Vietnam, as the British authorities in Hong Kong perceive them to be interested only in improving their standard of living rather than escaping persecution. This case perhaps demonstrates the difficulties of isolating social from other factors.

145

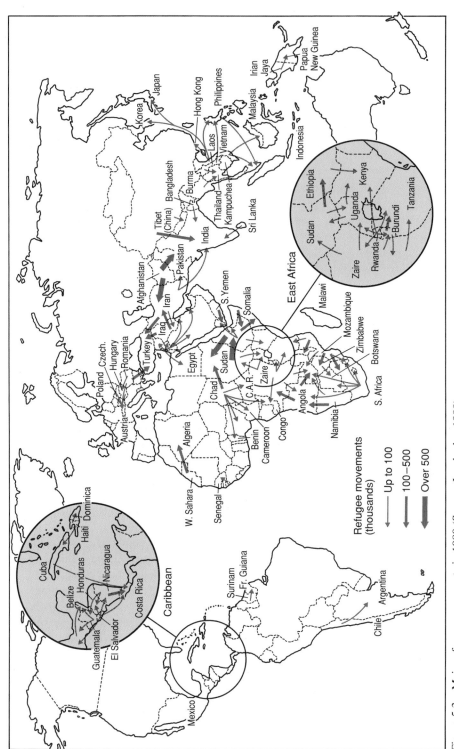

Figure 5.3 Main refugee movements in 1989 (Source: Leatherby, 1989)

3. Ecological factors

Environmental crises such as droughts, desertification and industrial accidents can have profound impacts on human migration. Environmental or ecological refugees have become the single largest class of displaced people in the world.

Industrial accidents can force thousands of people to migrate. Between 1960 and 1978 there were seven major chemical accidents worldwide, forcing almost 20 000 people to leave their homes. From 1978 to 1986 there were thirteen major chemical accidents, necessitating the evacuation of nearly one million people. The worst of these accidents occurred in 1984 at the Union Carbide pesticide plant in Bhopal, India, killing 2500 people and forcing 200 000 people to leave their homes. In some cases, such as Bhopal, human displacement is temporary, in others it may be permanent. The accident in 1986 at the Chernobyl nuclear power station in the USSR rendered an area of 2600 square kilometres uninhabitable due to radioactive contamination, necessitating the permanent evacuation of over 100 000 people.

The most widespread environmental threat at present is the deterioration of soils and vegetation. Desertification (literally the making of deserts) is the most severe form of land degradation and affects millions of people. It is most acute in arid and

Plate 5.5   Many people are not just refugees from political turmoil, but also from ecological hazards. In 1984 at Korem Relief Camp in Ethiopia, refugees were escaping a war as well as a severe drought. The woman pictured has all her belongings with her and has made a shelter with a blanket. She waits, with thousands of others, for aid. (Photograph: Mark Edwards/ Still Pictures)

semi-arid regions. The UN estimate that 4.5 billion hectares around the world are in various stages of desertification. That represents approximately 35% of the earth's land area, which is home to 850 million people (one sixth of the world's population). Though most people affected live in the Third World, it is not a phenomenon restricted to the developing countries; today parts of western USA and Australia are similarly affected. In the 1930s a combination of land degradation and drought produced the Great Dust Bowl on the Great Plains of the USA, which forced thousands of people to leave their homes. This migration of people caused by a combination of economic and environmental factors was made famous by John Steinbeck in his novel *The Grapes of Wrath*.

It is estimated that over ten million people worldwide have been forced to migrate as a result of ecological factors. Three categories of people are affected. First, those people who are displaced temporarily because of a local disruption such as an avalanche, land slide or earthquake. Secondly there are those who migrate because environmental degradation has undermined their livelihood or has posed unacceptable risks to health. Thirdly there are those who resettle because land degradation has resulted in desertification or other permanent changes in their habitat.

Despite the increasing evidence that environmental decline and contamination is responsible for increasing numbers of population movements, most governments and international organisations do not recognise environmental degradation as a factor causing migration. The growing concern about such migrations has prompted the Indian government to insert a new category of migrations into its 1991 Census. The category gives respondents the opportunity to state that the reason for migration from their last place of residence was, 'natural calamities such as droughts, floods, etc.' Population geographers are only just beginning to recognise the importance of ecological factors in the migration process, and a great deal of research has yet to be done.

4. Behavioural factors

The decision to migrate ultimately depends on the individual. Individuals have different attributes and motivations and respond in varying ways to different stimuli. It is these varying responses to socio-economic and environmental factors that make migration patterns difficult to classify and predict, as does the fact that individual decisions concerning migration are made on information that has come through a perceptual filter (see Figure 5.4). The area in which an individual lives, works and socialises is usually well known and directly experienced. By contrast, information about far off places has to be filtered by an individual from a number of sources. Such information may be obtained from other individuals by word of mouth, by reading, or from the radio or television. Using this filtered, and by definition imperfect information, many migrants make critical decisions concerning their future lives.

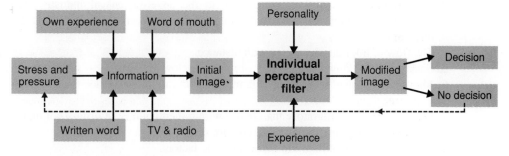

Figure 5.4 Role of the individual's perceptual filter in the decision-making process

ASSIGNMENTS
1. *(a) Study Figure 5.2. List the areas of origin of immigrants to i) Great Britain and ii) West Germany.*
   (b) Comment on the nature of and reasons for differences.
2. *(a) Using Figure 5.3 identify the main regions of refugee movement.*
   (b) Giving examples, compile a list of factors that may result in refugee movements.
   (c) What role do ecological factors have in initiating migration?
3. *With reference to Figures 5.1 and 5.4 discuss the role of individual perception in the decision to migrate.*

C. Theories of Migration

Unfortunately there is no comprehensive theory of migration which takes into account all the factors discussed above. Most theories stress socio-economic factors or behavioural inputs and ignore ecological factors. One of the earliest treaties concerning migration was put forward by E.G. Ravenstein in 1885 in what he called *The laws of migration.*

1. Ravenstein's Laws of Migration

Broad theories concerning the characteristics of migrants and their origins and destinations were formulated by Ravenstein in 1885 and 1889. These were published in response to a statement by a contemporary demographer that *migration appeared to lack any definite law.* Using data from the 1881 British census, Ravenstein formulated a series of laws which he believed explained contemporary migration in Europe. The main elements of his thesis are summarised below:
1. Most migrants move only a short distance, in a step by step progression.
2. The direction of migration is mainly from agricultural to industrial areas, therefore migrants are more likely to have rural origins than urban origins.

3. The volume of migration increases with the development of industry and commerce. The large industrial and commercial cities receive most long distance migrants.
4. The flow of migrants decreases with distance.
5. Each migration flow has a counter or returning flow.
6. Migrants are usually adults, with families rarely migrating outside their country of origin.
7. Females are more migratory than males within their country of origin, but males are more likely to migrate to other countries.
8. The major causes of migration are economic factors.

It should be remembered that Ravenstein's Laws were developed in and applied to Victorian Britain and were published at a time of rapid industrialisation which was accompanied by massive urban growth. Both industrialisation and urban growth were fuelled by rural to urban migration. It is perhaps for these reasons that he concludes that the major causes of migration were economic, that migration is selective and is also related to distance. These observations have become the basis of much subsequent work on migration.

2. Migration and distance

(a) Gravity model

Ravenstein very clearly stated that the volume of migration was inversely related to distance. This phenomenon is called *distance decay* and is analogous to Newton's physical law of universal gravitation. When applied to human population movements this law states that two places interact with each other in proportion to the product of their masses (measured by population numbers or job opportunities) and inversely according to distance (which can be measured in physical, time or cost terms). Such an explanation of population movement using the laws of gravity is known as the *Gravity Model*, and can be expressed using the following equation:

$$Mij = \frac{PiPj}{Dij}$$

M Migration   *P* Population
D Distance   *i, j* Settlements
Migration between settlement *i* and settlement *j* is the result of the multiplication of the populations of *i* and *j*, divided by the distance between *i* and *j*.

The Gravity Model theory is highly simplified since it assumes that (i) each migrant has the same information available and (ii) movement costs are the same in all directions. The decision-making process of the individual migrant is in effect reduced to a consideration of distance only. Distance is obviously only one of the many factors considered by potential migrants. Factors such as employment opportunities, the provision of housing and the level and quality of services also

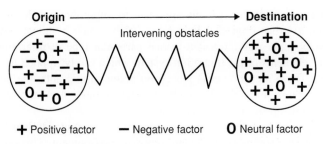

Origin ———————————————→ **Destination**

Intervening obstacles

+ Positive factor   **—** Negative factor   **O** Neutral factor

Figure 5.5   The intervening obstacle theory of migration (Source: Lee, 1966 in Ogden, 1984)

need to be included. Despite its limitations as a model of migrant behaviour the Gravity Model theory has been refined by many scholars and is still widely used.

(b) Intervening opportunities and obstacles

The relationship between distance and the volume of migration was taken a step further in the 1940s and 1950s by the American sociologist, S.A. Stouffer. He suggested that it was not distance itself which affected the volume of migrants, but the number of intervening opportunities. The decline in the number of migrants moving long distances, he claimed, was the result of the increasing number of opportunities that were presented to the migrant between origin and anticipated destination. These opportunities may include better housing, educational and healthcare facilities as well as superior employment opportunities. As distance increases so will the number of these intervening socio-economic opportunities, encouraging migrants to settle before they reach their hoped-for destination and thus reducing the flows.

In 1966 these ideas were further refined by American geographer E.S. Lee, who suggested that the obstacles to migration modified the process outlined by Stouffer (see Figure 5.5). Obstacles to migration may include distance and the cost of transportation, but may also comprise legal constraints, such as political boundaries, immigration laws and migration quotas. Lee thus broadened migration theory from the notion that migration is determined purely by distance and economic opportunity.

3. A systems approach

In an attempt to move away from these rather over-simplified theories of migration, geographers have increasingly moved towards a systems approach. The aim is to set migration in its social and economic context, as part of an interrelated system. Migration is viewed as a circular, interdependent and self-regulating system, in which the effects of changes in one part can have an impact on the whole system. All systems operate within an economic, social, political and technological environment, which is constantly changing. This approach can accommodate such changes and attempt to explain them.

151

The best example of the systems approach to migration is A.K. Mabogunje's study of rural-to-urban migration in Africa (1970), which is shown in Figure 5.6. Although Mabogunje was interested in one particular type of migration, he does identify three elements of the migration system which can be applied to other types of migration. These are: the stress placed on potential migrants; the controls that operate on migrants; and the adjustments that have to take place at both origin and destination following successful migration.

In Mabogunje's example the potential migrant is encouraged to leave the village by stimuli from the socio-economic and physical environment. This could include land scarcity and the attraction of the city and its opportunities, as well as the need for cash. Once the migrant has decided to leave the village two *control sub-systems* begin to operate. These control sub-systems comprise institutional forces both in the rural and urban areas. They may include the influence of the rural family and local community (encouraging or discouraging migration) as well as new friends and employers in the city who may affect the degree to which the migrant assimilates into the new environment. Once the movement has taken place, adjustment

Figure 5.6   A systems model of rural-to-urban migration in Africa

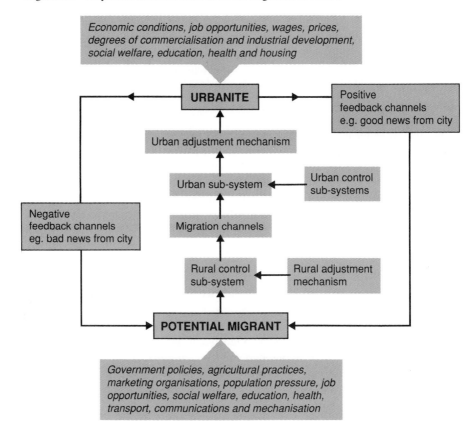

mechanisms come into play, both in the village and city. The rural family and community have to adjust to one fewer member of the social and agricultural system, whilst the city has to adjust to an addition to its labour force, and a burden on its services. Even when the migrant has successfully moved to the city, the system can still be affected, as the migrant sends back information to the village. This information may be positive, which in turn will encourage further migrations, or alternatively it may be negative, in which case the flow of migrants may be reduced.

The systems approach demonstrates that migration is part of an interlocking series of causes and effects. It highlights the self-modifying nature of the migration system and emphasises the effect of migration on the areas of origin and destination. It is an approach that is capable of taking account of all factors affecting migration.

4. The behavioural explanation

The theories discussed so far fail to suggest how individuals arrive at their decision to migrate and why certain categories of people are more likely to migrate. Behavioural geographers view the movement of people as a form of adaptation to stress. This includes internal stress comprising individual needs and aspirations, as well as external stress, such as the size of house, the nature of the neighbourhood and general environmental considerations. A behavioural analysis assumes that decision-making is a function of two processes, firstly the quantity and quality of perceived information available to the potential migrant, and secondly, the ability of the migrant to use such information. These processes are in turn the result of the socio-economic and physical environment in which migration occurs. Thus migrants are not random samples of the population but are necessarily selected. This selection occurs through individual information filters, but also by the migrants' ability to overcome stress as well as physical and legal constraints.

Although often used in migration analysis, the behavioural approach has one serious flaw. It assumes that all decisions to migrate are made freely. It neglects to recognise that there is a wide variety of constraints, including physical, economic and social as well as legal constraints upon migration, which operate in all societies. It can therefore be regarded as only a partial explanation of migration patterns.

ASSIGNMENTS

1. (a) Using data given in Table 5.1 and Figure 5.7 as a base map, plot the percentage change of population in England and Wales between 1981 and 1986.
   (b) Describe the patterns shown.
   (c) Where have most changes taken place?
   (d) Suggest reasons for these changes.
   (e) Do the trends shown confirm or refute any of Ravenstein's Laws of Migration?
2. Using Mabogunje's example, explain how the systems approach accommodates other theories of migration.

Table 5.1   Percentage population change in England and Wales, 1981–1986 (Source: OPCS)

	% change 1981–86
Metropolitan countries	
Tyne & Wear	−1.7
West Yorkshire	−0.7
South Yorkshire	−1.5
Greater Manchester	−1.5
Merseyside	−3.6
West Midlands	−1.5
Greater London	−0.4
Total	−1.7
Non-metropolitan regions	
North	−1.2
Yorkshire & Humberside	−0.4
North-West	−1.3
East Midlands	1.7
West Midlands	−0.1
South-West	3.7
East Anglia	5.1
South-East	2.8
Total	2.3
Wales	0.3

D. Consequences of Migration

The consequences of migration are complex, depending on the type of migration involved. Nevertheless, all migrations affect the economic and social systems of both origin and destination, as well as influencing the migrant as an individual. Most work on the consequences of migration has concentrated on the impact of labour migration, especially that of international movements. Although the following discussion stresses the consequences of labour migration, many of the consequences apply to other types of movement.

1. The impact on the area of origin

(a) Economic consequences

(i) *Remittances.* Labour migration is often regarded as the most economically beneficial form of migration to the area of origin. This is due to the remittances that labour migrants send to their families who remain in the area of origin. Taken

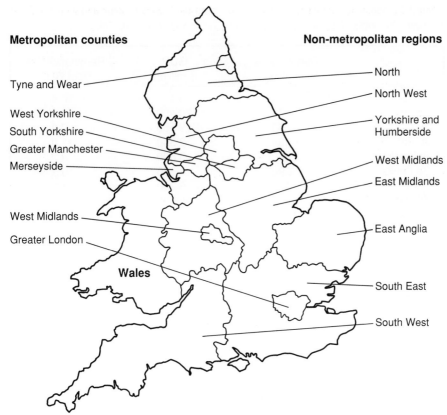

Metropolitan counties

Tyne and Wear

West Yorkshire
South Yorkshire
Greater Manchester
Merseyside

West Midlands

Greater London

Wales

Non-metropolitan regions

North

North West

Yorkshire and
Humberside

West Midlands

East Midlands

East Anglia

South East

South West

Figure 5.7   Outline map of metropolitan and non-metropolitan regions of England and Wales (Source: OPCS)

at a national scale these remittances can be very substantial. Table 5.2 shows the amount of money in the form of official remittances sent back to countries of origin. For a number of countries remittances are a very important form of income. For example, official remittances in Pakistan and Yemen PDR amount to the equivalent of over 65% of Gross Domestic Product. This figure does not include the large sums of money unofficially remitted, either in the form of cash or goods.

Remittances can have negative economic effects in the area of origin. For example, agricultural production may be adversely affected, not only because of the loss of labour, but also because regular remittances mean that rural families are no longer dependent on their farms. This has occurred in Yemen PDR where large areas of land are no longer farmed. It has also been accompanied by a trend to buy imported foodstuffs. In Egypt and Sudan there is a consumer move away from locally produced maize flour to imported fine white wheat flour. A study of the use of remittances in Portugal showed that 32% of remittances were spent on consumer items and domestic appliances, 24% on children's education and 38% on land and housing. A study on remittances in Mexico produced similar findings, with 72%

155

Table 5.2   Value of migrant remittances through official channels compared with Gross Domestic Product (GDP) of selected countries, 1982 (Source: Owen, 1985)

	Remittances $ million	GDP $ million	Remittances as % of GDP
Bangladesh	329	3 170	10.4
Egypt	2 074	26 400	7.8
India	2 293	29 550	7.8
Jordan	1 084	3 500	31.0
Pakistan	2 580	3 500	73.7
Sri Lanka	290	1 500	19.3
Sudan	131	9 290	1.4
Thailand	616	36 790	1.7
Turkey	2 187	49 980	4.4
Yemen PDR	411	630	65.2
Yemen AR	1 118	3 210	34.8

of remittances spent on immediate consumer items, 9% on housing and only 7% on economically productive projects. This implies that remittances are not spent on the support of local agricultural and industrial production but are used to buy imported goods. They have also allowed the privatisation of basic services which cannot meet local demands, such as education and health care. Remittances have also invariably meant that the price of land has increased in many areas of origin.

(ii) *Role in development*. One of the major criticisms of labour migration is that it has failed to provide any discernable development impetus in the areas of origin. Any capital that is used in this way is primarily invested in mechanising agricultural production, in tourist-related infrastructure or in small service enterprises, such as small shops, garages or taxis. Returning migrants with newly acquired skills may provide a catalyst for modernisation, though this is largely unproven. Destination countries are not usually in need of skilled workers; instead they need workers to perform repetitive tasks at the lower end of the industrial hierarchy. It is therefore not in the interest of employers to offer immigrants skill enhancement opportunities or formal technical training. Even if a migrant did acquire skills, evidence suggests that returning migrants do not aspire to work in the industrial sector.

One attempt to assess the balance of economic advantage and disadvantage on a major labour exporting country is S.J. Burki's study of Pakistan (1985). The conclusions of his study showed that as a result of labour migration and remittances, the Pakistan economy grew at a rate of 5% per annum throughout the 1970s, rather than an estimated 2% if migration had not occurred. The migrants themselves created markets overseas for Pakistani-produced goods, which stimulated domestic production. However, on the negative side 5% of the national labour force was lost, with the additional cost of training replacements. The attendant labour shortage contributed to local wage rises and the desire to spend remittances on land pushed prices up, resulting in increased inflation. Nevertheless, Burki concludes that the economic impact of labour migration on Pakistan is a positive one.

In many instances labour migration provides clear financial benefits to the area of origin and specifically to the migrant's family, although these are often exaggerated. These economic gains must, however, be weighed against the social impact of such migration.

(b) Social consequences

Depopulation of areas of origin can be a harmful legacy of migration. In most situations of out-migration it is the young and very often the innovators who leave first. This leaves a community of older, more conservative members who are less receptive to new ideas. Not only was this the case in nineteenth-century Ireland, but it appears to be the case in many less developed regions now experiencing out-movements. The result is a skewed age and sex structure which has serious implications for social welfare systems. Not only does depopulation have demographic implications, it also has serious social consequences. The loss of young adults may result in the disintegration of traditional social and political life and may assist the erosion of service infrastructure (see Figure 5.8). For example, due to falling population numbers schools may be closed, similarly banks, shops, post offices and doctors' surgeries may disappear, even public transport facilities may be cut. This very often results in severe deprivation in rural areas of out-migration.

Plate 5.6   Rural depopulation in Great Britain often results in the closure of rural services such as schools and post offices. In this Lincolnshire village both the school and the telephone exchange have been closed and converted into residential properties. (Photograph: L.P. Barrett)

157

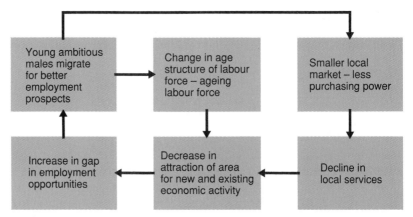

Figure 5.8   Rural depopulation and its socio-economic impact (Source: Vaughan-William, P. *Brasil*, 1981, University Tutorial Press, now Unwin Hyman of HarperCollins Publishers Limited)

2. The impact on the area of destination

(a) Economic consequences

The impact of migration on areas of destination can be as complex as the impact on areas of origin. The most frequently quoted economic advantage of labour migration is the supply of cheap labour. The German economist Professor Rüstow recently calculated that in 1966 a foreign worker's output in West Germany was worth about DM27 000, of which DM19 000 was paid out in wages. West German industry and the nation's economy clearly benefited from the use of imported labour. The French economy also benefits from its migrant workers. It is estimated that the French economy has benefited to the tune of 375 million francs from its Algerian workers alone. An indirect result of the influx of foreign workers may be the depression of local wages and the undermining of trades unions, which is seen as beneficial by many industrialists and governments.

The economies of countries of destination clearly benefit from the importation of labour. There are, however, costs. Migrants must be supplied with housing and if their families accompany them, educational and healthcare facilities must be provided. Nevertheless, the economic advantages to the areas of destination on the whole are positive.

(b) Social consequences

Due to the selective nature of labour migration, there is inevitably a demographic imbalance in areas of migration. The newcomers usually include large numbers of male adults, who may after a while choose to bring their young families with them. The demographic result of this type of movement is illustrated by Figure 5.9a, where the unbalanced demographic nature of Turkish migration to The Netherlands in 1976 is shown. As migration becomes long-term and permanent and family

a) 1st January 1976

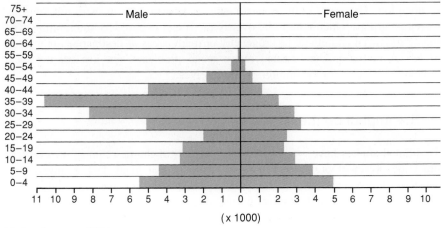

b) 1st January 1981

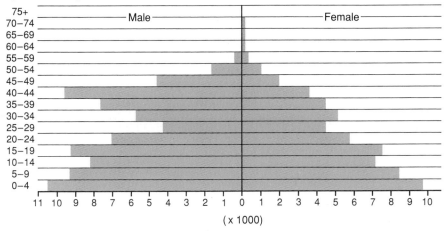

Figure 5.9 Foreigners in the Netherlands with Turkish nationality, by age and sex, 1976–1981 (Source: Van Amersfoort *et al*, 1984)

regroupment takes place, the demographic imbalance is ironed out. Figure 5.9b shows the population pyramid of Turkish immigrants in The Netherlands in 1981. Whatever the length of stay, labour migrants clearly put demands on the social service provisions of the host regions. A pressing problem in many host societies is the education of the children of migrants, many of whom have only a tenuous social and economic place in their country of residence. Increasingly, host societies are having to provide special educational facilities for these children.

Migration invariably involves the establishment of new cultural groups in the areas of destination. This can be seen as an enhancement to the host society, but can also present problems. Migrants who stay for extended periods become more assertive of their economic, political and social rights, which may invoke a reaction by local people who perceive the newcomers as representing social and economic competition. The result in many host countries has been the growth of right-wing extremist groups which tend to be overtly racist and opposed to immigration. The increasing racial and ethnic heterogeneity of many areas of destination, as a result of labour migration, has created many social problems, not just for the local population but also for the immigrants themselves.

3. The impact on the migrant

Traditional studies have emphasised the isolation of the newcomer, who is very often the object of prejudice. There is no doubt that many labour migrants to Western Europe since 1945 have experienced discrimination and even violence. In 1972, for example, Dutch workers burned down the lodging houses of immigrant workers in Rotterdam. In France there have been periodic attacks on Algerian workers, whose headquarters in Paris, Lyon and Roubaix were bombed in July 1975. Attacks have also taken place in other European countries. It not surprising, therefore, to find that a number of studies have identified a relationship between migration and family disorganisation, mental illness, delinquency and poverty. This relationship, it is suggested, is the result not only of aggravated hostility and prejudice, but also of a lack of a supportive receiving population. The importance to a newcomer of a receptive, culturally similar group cannot be over-emphasised. It can help migrants adapt to their new environments, thereby minimising the effect of a dramatic transition that requires a complete re-organisation of the life of a migrant.

In most situations a migrant has to adapt to a new social, economic and political environment. On arriving at the area of destination the migrant goes through three inter-related processes. First, acculturation must take place. Secondly, the migrant must adjust to the new economic and social environment. Thirdly, the migrant must participate in the institutional and social groupings of the new environment. The success at these three processes will determine whether a migrant will eventually conform to and assimilate into the host community or will choose to live in a distinct spatial group. For example, many of the early migrants to the UK from the Commonwealth choose to live in spatially segregated areas of inner cities. Figure 5.10 shows the distribution of immigrants from the new commonwealth in the city of Birmingham. Originally the reason for this segregation may have been prejudice and poverty. Today, however, an important reason for these cultural groupings is social cohesion.

ASSIGNMENTS

1. *(a) Using Table 5.2 assess the importance of remittances to areas of out-migration.*
   (b) List the costs and benefits of remittances to areas of origin.
   (c) What are the social consequences of out-migration on the area of origin (see Figure 5.8)?
2. *(a) Analyse the economic costs and benefits of migration to the areas of destination.*

160

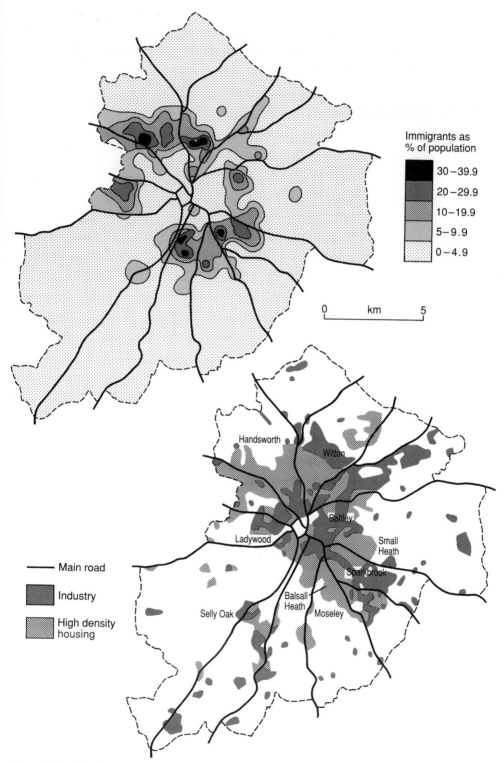

Figure 5.10   Spatial distribution of people born in the New Commonwealth living in Birmingham, 1966

161

(b) Describe the age and sex structure of Turkish immigrants to The
    Netherlands shown in Figure 5.9. Comment on the potential impact on the
    host community.

E. Case Studies

1. Rural-to-urban migration: the case of Brazil

(a) Reasons for migration

Although urbanisation has a long history in many parts of the world, for example
China, Greece and South Eastern Nigeria, many Third World regions have a smaller
proportion of people living in cities than other parts of the world. Figure 5.11
shows that Africa and Asia are the least urbanised regions, in contrast to North

Figure 5.11   Urban population as a percentage of total population, by major world region,
1950–1990

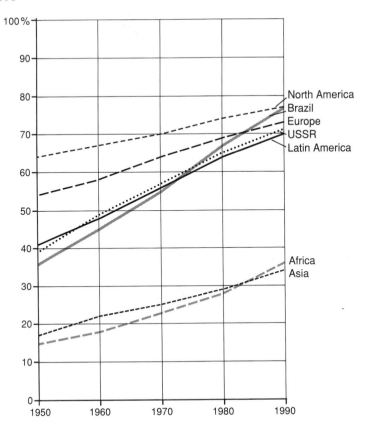

America where over 75% of the population are urban dwellers. Although less urbanised, the Third World and particularly Latin America, is experiencing the highest global rates of urban growth.

Latin America is a region that has experienced rapid and sustained urban growth since 1950. In that year less than half the population of the region lived in cities. However, by 1980 the proportion of Latin American urban dwellers equalled that of the USSR and was only 4% less than in Europe. Within Latin America, Uruguay has the highest proportion of urban population (87% in 1987), followed by Argentina and Chile (84%), Venezuela (76%) and Brazil (73%). In 1988, 220 million people in the region lived in cities, with Sao Paulo (19.9 million), Rio de Janerio (14.7) and Buenos Aires (11.5) ranked amongst the world's most populated cities.

Brazil, with an area of 8512 square kilometres and a population of 142 million (1987), is the largest country in Latin America. In 1987, 75% of the Brazilian population lived in cities, representing a rapid change from rural to urban living that is shown in Figure 5.11. Since 1950 the rate of growth in the rural population

Figure 5.12   Population change in Brazil, by state, 1970–1980 (Source: Vaughan-Williams, 1981)

Figure 5.12a) Rural population increase (%)

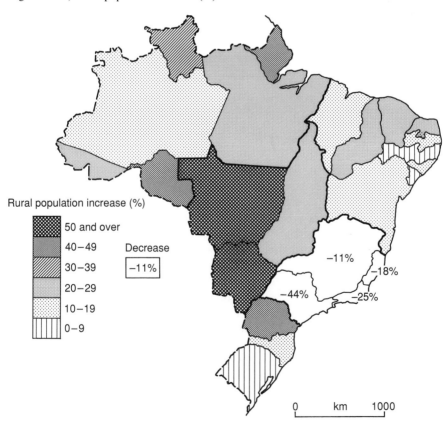

163

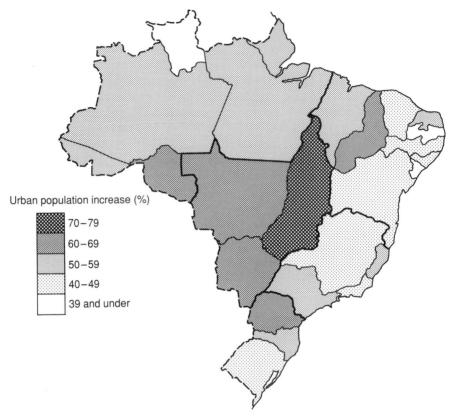

Urban population increase (%)

70–79
60–69
50–59
40–49
39 and under

Figure 5.12b) Urban population increase (%)

has declined steadily. Figure 5.12a shows the regional pattern of rural population change between 1970 and 1980. The map indicates that four states in the south eastern part of the country experienced negative growth rates, whereas the peripheral states of Parana, Mato Grosso, Rondonia and Amapa all experienced growth rates of over 40%. The rate of urban population growth shown in Figure 5.12b is, by contrast, much higher, with the growth rate exceeding 38% in all states. The states with the highest rural population growth rates also recorded high urban growth rates. This can be explained by the fact that these states are all areas where the Brazilian government is encouraging frontier migration through regional development programmes and colonisation projects. These include the *opening up* of forested areas by the construction of roads, including the Belem-Brasilia highway and the Transamazonia highway, shown on Figure 5.13. In addition Brasilia was inaugurated as the new federal capital in 1960, attracting investment and migrants.

In the period 1970 to 1980 the rate of annual natural increase of the Brazilian population was 2.2%, higher than the average rural population growth rate of 1.6%. The average annual growth rate of the urban population over the same period was 5.2%, more than twice the natural rate of population increase. These figures indicate

Figure 5.12c) Administrative boundaries

that urban growth in Brazil is being fuelled by rural-to-urban migration. The two major metropolitan regions in the country are Sao Paulo and Rio de Janerio in the south eastern part of the country. It is principally these two cities that act as magnets to the migrant.

Flows of rural migrants to cities are caused by inter-related environmental, historical, economic, social and political factors, which are usually explained by push-pull factors. The movement of large numbers of migrants to Brazil's cities can be explained by a set of negative factors operating in rural areas, *pushing* people to leave, whilst at the same time the perceived benefits of life in the city are *pulling* potential migrants. The components of such push-pull factors for Latin America are shown in Table 5.3. These movements have been facilitated by improvements in interregional transport networks and systems. As Figure 5.13 shows, Brazil has more than 16 000 kilometres of roads, all of which make the movement from rural to urban areas faster, cheaper and more comfortable.

The largest interregional movement in Brazil in the last forty years has been the loss of people from the north eastern regions to Sao Paulo. As outlined in section B, movements of this type can be explained by economic and environmental factors.

Figure 5.13   Brazilian road system, 1987 (Source: Morris, 1987)

The land ownership pattern for much of Brazil is two-fold. First, large areas of land are held by a small percentage of the population, in large estates, and secondly, small plots of land are cultivated by the majority of people. The first type of farming known as *latifundios* (up to 20 000 ha) is usually extensively managed, requiring little labour input. The rest of the land is farmed intensively in small farm units known as *minifundios* (averaging 2 ha), by either family owners, tenants or share croppers. The areas farmed are usually too small to provide an income, or employment for the local rural population. Approximately 32% of farms in north eastern Brazil are much less than 10 hectares in area, with a further 35% between 10 and 50 hectares, covering in total only 10.5% of the land area. Restricted access to land in combination with recurrent droughts and environmental degradation, are seen by many as major push factors in rural-to-urban migration in Latin America.

Widespread mass communications such as radio and television have raised the awareness of the Brazilian rural population of the opportunities available in the cities. Rural people often perceive urban areas as having better facilities: superior educational and medical opportunities as well as piped water and electricity. Modern communications have made rural people aware of large rural and urban differentials

Plate 5.7 Poor landless peasants in the North East of Brazil have the choice of either taking low paid casual jobs on large plantation estates, as pictured, or migrating to the city. (Photograph: Paul Harrison/Panos Pictures)

in living standards. This difference was borne out by a survey that suggested that 73% of rural households do not have access to minimum goods and services, whereas in urban areas the proportion of poor households is 35%. The percentage of households classified as destitute, defined as households without a minimal diet, shows a similar differential: 42% of rural families are classed as destitute, but only 15% of urban households. Thus the perceived differences between rural and urban areas in terms of living standards appear to be borne out in reality. Many rural people move to the city in the hope of achieving material benefits for themselves and their children.

However, the actual opportunities available to urban in-migrants are often very different from the mental images they have built up. Urban in-migrants usually begin their urban lives in over-crowded shanty towns which lack basic services, utilities, and amenities, including sanitation, water supply and educational and medical facilities. These areas have high disease and infant mortality rates. New migrants may also experience difficulties in finding employment, and often have no choice but to work long hours in poor conditions in local manufacturing enterprises. Many rural-to-urban migrants and their families experience severe poverty. Alternatively they may enter the informal economy (for example as shoe shiners or petty traders), or turn to crime, such as illicit brewing or prostitution.

Table 5.3   Push-pull factors operating in Latin American rural to urban migration (Source: Butterworth & Chance, 1981)

Force	Structural	Individual
Push	Type of land holding (latifundio, minifundio)	Lack of skills
	Insufficient or poor land; uneconomical exploitation of resources	Boredom, loneliness
	Lack of alternative employment	
	Absence of sanitation and medical facilities	
	Lack of transportation improvements	
	Violence	
	Poor educational facilities	
	Rudimentary communications	
	Mechanisation and commercialisation of agriculture	
	External markets	
	Poverty	
Pull	Employment opportunities	Chance of advancement
	Health and medical services	Presence of relatives
	Transportation	Bright lights and adventure
	Educational facilities	Rising expectations (all categories)

(b) Selectivity of migration

Rural-to-urban migration in Latin America, as in other parts of the world, is age and sex selective. In this region as elsewhere it is usually young adults who migrate to the city, leaving the middle-aged and elderly behind in the rural areas. However, in terms of gender selectivity Latin America differs from other regions. It is generally accepted that males are more migratory than females, and in Africa and Asia this is certainly the case; however, in Latin America, rural-to-urban migration is dominated by women. Again, this pattern can be explained by push-pull factors.

Women in Latin America have relatively low rates of participation in the agricultural labour force, estimated at 20%. (In African countries the figure for female agriculture participation rate varies from over 40% to as high as 80%.) The capitalisation of agriculture since 1950 has meant that rural employment opportunities have declined markedly, especially for women. At the same time the opportunities for female employment in the service and industrial sectors of the cities have been increasing. In Brazil, for example, 31% of all urban women between the ages of 15 and 69 are classed as employed, whereas the figure for rural women is only 17%. There are clearly greater economic opportunities for women in the cities, particularly in domestic service and other unskilled tertiary occupations. Over a third of the Brazilian female labour force outside agriculture is employed in domestic service.

Plate 5.8   This picture of a shanty housing area of La Paz in Bolivia, shows the type of makeshift housing and poor conditions that await most rural-to-urban migrants in Latin America. (Photograph: Sean Sprague/Panos Pictures)

The consequence of push and pull factors in Latin America, and especially in Brazil, has been the movement of large numbers of rural women to urban areas seeking employment. The result is high female to male ratios in the cities. In 1975 there were approximately 109 women to every 100 men in Latin American cities (in Africa where male migration is the norm the proportions were 92 women to every 100 men). Thus the concept of push-pull can be used not only to explain rural-to-urban migration in total, but also to explain the selectivity of such movements.

2. Government policy and migration: the case of Turkish labour migrants

The role of government policies in regulating migration flows has intensified since 1945, and has a significant effect on patterns of labour migration. Figure 5.14 is a simple model of the international labour migration process. The model demonstrates that both labour immigration and return migration is very much dependent on economic and political factors in both areas of origin and destination. Factors such as the availability of jobs and favourable legislation dictate flows of labour migrants, as is demonstrated by the example of Turkish labour migration.

169

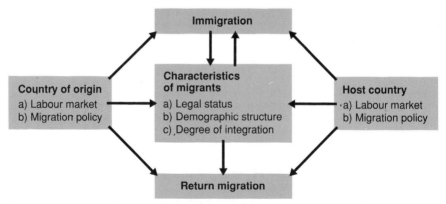

Figure 5.14   Model of the international labour migration process (Source: Van Amersfoort *et al*, 1984)

Plate 5.9   In the early 1970s almost 80% of Turks employed abroad were working in West Germany, usually employed in semi or unskilled jobs. In this photograph Turkish workers lay tarred roads in West Berlin. (Photograph: Donna Binder/LINK)

Large-scale emigration from Turkey only began in the early 1960s. At this time high rates of demographic growth combined with the mechanisation of agriculture, led to continuously high levels of unemployment. The Turkish government through the Turkish Employment Service encouraged the export of this surplus labour, by way of bi-lateral labour agreements. Turkey signed its first bi-lateral labour agreement with West Germany in 1961, followed by treaties with Austria in 1964,

France in 1966, Sweden in 1967 and Australia in 1967. Labour shortages in Western Europe during the 1960s motivated European governments to sign bi-lateral labour agreements. These inter-state contracts proved to be instrumental in determining which nationalities entered a specific labour market.

Until the mid-1970s Turkish migration was aimed towards Western Europe, and especially West Germany. Turkish migrants were more numerous in West Germany than any other European country. In 1963, over 22 000 Turks were employed in West Germany, by 1973 this figure had increased to over 615 000. So significant was this flow that in 1973, 78% of all Turks employed abroad were working in West Germany. At first this flow consisted of young men, but after 1967 the number of Turkish women seeking employment increased. By 1973 women accounted for 22% of all migrant workers in West Germany.

The boom in the European economies ended in the early 1970s with economic recession, and rising unemployment. This led to dramatic changes in immigration policies. West Germany banned the entry of workers from outside the EC in November 1973. France followed a year later, and most Western European countries also introduced similar restrictive policies. Figure 5.15 demonstrates the dramatic impact this legislation had on Turkish immigration. Between 1973 and 1975, Turkish immigration to West Germany dropped by almost 60%. Return migration also increased at this time, perhaps illustrating the difficulties experienced by Turkish immigrants in securing employment.

Labour migration from Turkey to Western Europe therefore practically ceased from the mid-1970s. However, immigration to West Germany has continued, as

Figure 5.15   Migration of Turkish nationals to West Germany, 1965–1982 (Source: Van Amersfoort *et al*, 1984)

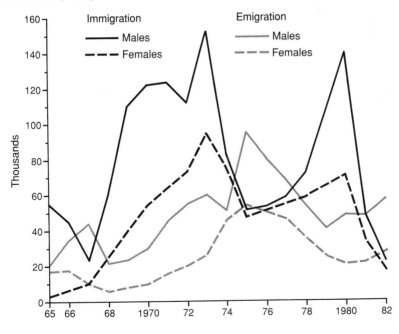

Figure 5.15 shows. This is due to family regroupment and natural increase. There is a clear eight-year gap between the two immigration peaks on Figure 5.15. This reflects West German legislation concerning permanent residence permits, which are only given after eight years residence in West Germany. By 1982 Turkish immigration to West Germany was at a very low level, illustrating the effectiveness of state regulation.

Since the mid-1970s the direction of recorded flow of Turkish labour migration has changed from Western Europe to the Middle East. This flow reached a peak in 1981 when 95% of all departures from Turkey were to three Arab countries, namely Iraq, Libya and Saudi Arabia. By 1984 almost all Turkish departures were to these three destinations. These flows can be explained by the large number of Turkish companies that have won contracts in the region, mainly in the construction industry. Workers are attracted to these countries by high wages, and are mainly skilled men, who sign short duration contracts of up to three years. These men have few legal rights and family regroupment is discouraged. Once the construction boom is completed in these oil rich countries, Turkish labour will have to find a new destination.

ASSIGNMENTS

1. (a) Describe the pattern shown on Figure 5.12a. Which regions are gaining/ losing rural population?
   (b) Using 5.12b examine the pattern of urban population growth.
   (c) Suggest reasons for these trends.
   (d) Explain why women dominate the rural-to-urban flow of migration in Latin America.
2. (a) The case of Turkey demonstrates the importance of government bi-lateral labour agreements in determining flows of migrants. Explain how legislation accounts for the patterns shown in Figure 5.15.
   (b) Do any of the theories discussed in Section C adequately explain this type of migration?

Key Ideas

Introduction

1. Side by side with fertility and mortality, migration is the third component of population change.
2. Migration is difficult to define, but usually involves a permanent or semi-permanent change in residence of twelve months or more. It is not to be confused with circulation.

A. Types of migration

1. It is very difficult to classify migration, but geographers usually favour the criteria of distance, time or area of origin, or some combination of these three.

172

B. Factors affecting migration

1. It is not easy to isolate and distinguish the factors affecting migration. However, it is usually recognised that economic, social and ecological factors are important.
2. Economic factors are often regarded as the main reasons for migrations, with labour migration being the major manifestation of this type of motive. Labour migration is selective in nature and may be long or short term. The major destinations of labour migrants since 1945 are Western Europe and the Gulf States.
3. Social pressures can also produce migration flows, as evidenced by the 14.5 million official refugees worldwide in 1989.
4. Ecological decline can also result in the movement of people. It is estimated that over 10 million people globally have moved as a result of environmental pressures.
5. The decision to migrate is a response to varying stimuli, which are processed through an individual's perceptual filter. The response to such information helps explain why certain categories of people choose to migrate, and others facing the same pressures do not.

C. Theories of migration

1. There is no comprehensive theory of migration, but E.G. Ravenstein is credited with producing the first treatise concerning migration. His *Laws of Migration* (1885,1889) have become the basis of migration theory.
2. The Gravity Model, based on Newton's physical law of universal gravitation, stresses the importance of distance in determining migration flows.
3. S.A. Stouffer suggested that it was not only distance that affected the volume of migration, but the number of *intervening opportunities* that presented themselves to the migrant.
4. Stouffer's work was modified by E.S. Lee in 1966 who suggested that *intervening obstacles* as well as opportunities must be considered in any analysis of migration flows.
5. The systems approach to migration views migration as a circular, interdependent and self-regulating system, in which changes in one part of the system can have an impact on the whole system. This is demonstrated using A.K. Mabogunje's (1970) study of rural-to-urban migration in West Africa.
6. The behavioural explanation of migration views movement as the result of the individual's ability to overcome and adapt to internal and external stress. This is dependent on the socio-economic environment in which decisions are being made.

D. Consequences of migration

1. The consequences of migration are complex, affecting the economic and social systems of both areas of origin and destination.

2. The economic consequences on the area of origin (involving the sending of remittances), are usually regarded as positive, although they can produce negative features such as inflated land prices and increased consumer spending on imported items.
3. Depopulation can be a serious consequence of migration in areas of origin, with young innovators often being the first to leave.
4. The economic impact on areas of destination is seen on the whole to be positive, although there are costs involved, such as the provision of housing and other services to migrants and their families.
5. The social consequences of migration on destination areas are debatable. The establishing of new cultural groups can produce cultural tensions but can also enhance the host community.
6. The impact of movement on the migrant often depends on the existence of a supportive receiving population and the ability of the migrant to adapt to the host community. Very often, however, migrants face prejudice and even violence.

E. Case Studies

1. Brazil is rapidly urbanising, principally through rural-to-urban migration. Movement can be explained by *push* factors operating in rural areas and *pull* factors attracting migrants in urban areas.
2. Migration in Brazil is age and gender selective, with large numbers of female migrants seeking domestic employment in the cities. This can be seen to be a response to the poor economic opportunities available to women in the rural areas.
3. The case of Turkish labour migration highlights the role of government policy in regulating migration flows. In the 1960s, after the signing of bi-lateral labour agreements, the principal flow of Turkish migration was to Western Europe. Following economic recession in the 1970s these countries tightened up their labour importing legislation, and the flow was reduced. The result in the 1980s was that the Middle East became the favoured destination of Turkish labour migrants, following the signing of labour agreements with these countries.

Additional Activities

1. (a) Identify ten recent in-migrants. They could be in your class, street, or neighbourhood. Ask them if they would be willing to answer a short questionnaire.
   (b) Devise and undertake a short questionnaire that will elicit the following information:
   i) where the migrant came from;
   ii) why he or she moved;

iii) how long he or she has been at this address;

iv) what have been the advantages of the move;

v) what have been the problems encountered in adapting to the new environment.

(c) Analyse (and summarise) your results using flow maps, histograms and tables.

(d) Discuss your results with reference to the theories of migration outlined in Section C of this chapter.

2. 'Labour migration represents a redistribution of human resources.' Discuss this statement, using examples.

3. With reference to Chapters 3 and 4 explain how migration can affect the population structure of both origin and host communities. In particular, note how age and gender bias can affect birth and death rates.

6 Population Planning Policies

Introduction

The social and economic impact of population growth has meant that governments have adopted policies which attempt to regulate both the size and distribution of population. Strictly defined, population planning policies are those measures instituted by a government which influence population size, growth and distribution. All governments have a population policy, even inaction is a policy choice which has population implications. As there is only limited scope for any manipulation of the death rate and the rate of international migration, it is the political intervention in fertility and population distribution that forms the core of most population policies.

A. Policies concerning Population Growth

Table 6.1 shows a selection of the types of policies that governments may choose to implement in an attempt to alter fertility patterns. Government laws concerning minimum age at marriage and children's schooling are direct ways in which governments can affect fertility. By contrast a government can alter the social and economic environment, which can in turn affect people's decisions concerning marriage and children. Such indirect means include tax programmes and targeted

Table 6.1   Government decisions which may alter population growth

Direct policies	Indirect policies
Policy and laws 1. Minimum marriage age 2. Women's status 3. Children's education and work 4. Breastfeeding 5. Number of children per family	Government spending 1. Education 2. Primary healthcare 3. Family planning 4. Incentives for fertility control 5. Old-age security Tax programmes 1. Family allowances 2. User fees for larger families

spending. Both direct and indirect policies alter birth rates by affecting the proximate determinants of fertility (biological factors) which are discussed in Chapter 4 (see Figure 4.7).

Many countries have laws that impinge on population. These laws concern marriage and divorce, contraception, sterilisation and abortion, maternity leave and grants, and length of schooling, as well as equal opportunities for women. However, most governments choose to alter fertility patterns by manipulating the socio-economic environment in which fertility decisions are made rather than by legislating directly. Recognising the economic importance of children to parents (see Wealth Flows Theory, Chapter 4), most governments use economic factors as incentives or disincentives to influence fertility decisions. For example, incentives to reduce fertility often involve compensating parents economically for the loss of not having a child. Disincentives can also raise the cost of rearing children in the anticipation of reducing fertility. Incentives to increase fertility may involve significant financial payouts to compensate for the mother's potential loss of earnings, whilst disincentives may involve restricting access to contraceptive advice. Couples must therefore decide between the possible rewards and penalties, imposed by government, of having children.

Government policy can thus be used to increase as well as decrease population growth. A policy designed to increase natural growth is called a *pro-natalist policy*, whilst a policy seeking to reduce population growth is known as an *anti-natalist policy*. A simple distinction can be made between the pro-natalist policies adopted by many developed and oil-rich countries, and the anti-natalist policies adopted by many Third World countries.

1.   Pro-natalist policies

A pro-natalist policy seeks to increase natural population growth and usually requires an increase in the birth rate. This can be achieved by restricting access to methods of fertility control such as contraceptives and abortion, and by providing financial incentives and a social climate that encourages large families. Pro-natalist policies are most strongly associated with fertility downturns in twentieth-century Europe.

France was the first of a number of Western European countries to be concerned by low birth rates in the inter-war period (1919–39). The decline in French fertility can be traced back to the period before the French Revolution and by the 1830s the CBR in France was below 30 per 1000. This decline in the French fertility rate continued steadily, reaching a figure of approximately 19 per 1000 by 1914. A concerned French government then introduced a number of measures designed to encourage fertility, culminating in July 1939 with the passing of the famous French *Code de la famille*. This was a complicated piece of pro-natalist legislation. The main provisions of the code consisted of cash incentives to mothers who stayed at home to care for their children and a system of graduated cash allowances. These allowances were initially fixed at 10% of the breadwinner's wage for the second child, increasing to 20% for each subsequent child. In 1941 this allowance was raised to 50% for the fourth and subsequent children. In addition there were provisions for home assistance for families, subsidised holidays, heavy penalties for practising abortion and the official banning of the sale of contraceptives (not repealed until 1967).

The French system tied economic incentives to wages. By contrast pre-war Germany adopted a system of state cash incentives and disincentives. In Nazi Germany after 1933, in an effort to increase the birth rate, marriage loans were payable to those of Aryan stock and of sound health. The loan was repayable over eight years, but a quarter of the loan would be cancelled on the birth of each child. In addition, free medical services were available to expectant mothers and small children. Families also received a regular family allowance. At the same time family planning clinics were closed down. The success of these pro-natalist measures is hard to evaluate because of the combined effects of other factors, but between 1933 and 1939 the German birth rate increased from 14.7 to 20.3 per 1000.

The post-war baby boom of the 1950s and early 1960s in Europe pushed government concern about fertility into the background. However, the fertility declines of the 1970s again created government concern, especially in the countries of Eastern Europe. It is in Eastern Europe that modern pro-natalist policies have been most stringent and most debatable. In the mid-1960s these countries exhibited the world's lowest CBRs of 15–16 per 1000, giving rise to concern about the future size of the labour force.

In Hungary the incentives for parents to increase their fertility were many, including monthly payments for children which were equivalent to about 12% of the average wage, generous maternity leave, a birth bonus payment, partial down payment for a house and subsidies on children's clothing, milk and school supplies. In addition, families were given extra paid holidays and mothers guaranteed job security. In 1974 restrictions were placed on legal abortions. The impact of this vast array of measures has been negligible. Fertility in Hungary has not increased, the fertility rate in 1987 was exactly the same as in 1965, standing at 1.8. Economic incentives to increase fertility in Hungary evidently do not off-set the increased private costs of larger families. The success of many pro-natalist policies can therefore be questioned.

2.   Anti-natalist policies

An anti-natalist policy seeks to reduce natural population increase, primarily through the reduction of births. This can be achieved by offering incentives to reduce fertility and by making family planning services available and affordable. Anti-natalist concern can be traced back to the mid-1960s when the publication of the results of the 1960s round of censuses revealed higher levels of population growth in the Third World than had been expected. It also coincided with the development of cheap and relatively efficient birth control methods such as oral contraceptives and intra-uterine devices (IUDs).

In 1952 India was the first government formally to support an anti-natalist policy. By 1964, Pakistan, South Korea, Fiji and China had implemented fertility control policies. By 1984 some 45 countries in the developing world had adopted

Table 6.2 Demographic targets of selected developing countries (Source: World Bank, 1984; 1989)

	Year	Policy target TFR	Policy target CBR	Rates in 1987 TFR	Rates in 1987 CBR
Bangladesh	2000	2.5	–	5.5	41
China	2000	2.0	–	2.4	21
India	1996	–	21	4.3	32
Indonesia	1990	2.7	22	3.5	29
Korea	1988	2.1	–	2.1	20
Nepal	2000	2.5	–	5.9	41
Pakistan	1988	–	36	6.7	47
Philippines	1987	–	28	3.9	30
Thailand	1986	2.6	–	2.8	25
Egypt	2000	–	20	4.8	36
Ghana	2000	3.3	–	6.4	46
Mauritius	1988	2.3	–	2.1	20
Tunisia	2001	–	22	4.1	30
Uganda	1995	5.0	–	6.9	50
Jamaica	2000	2.1	–	2.9	26
Mexico	1988	–	25	3.6	29

TFR   Total Fertility Rate   CBR   Crude Birth Rate

official policies aimed at reducing the rate of population growth. Many of these countries have set quantitative targets. Table 6.2 summarises the demographic targets for 16 countries in terms of either CBR or fertility rates, and compares them with current rates. Demographic targets vary between countries and are expressed in different ways. For example, Jamaica aims to reach population replacement

Plate 6.1   This traditional Indian family planning poster is promoting the two-child family. (Photograph: G. O'Hare)

levels by the years 2000. Ghana, on the other hand, hopes to reduce population growth by 2.0% by that date, and Uganda has set 2.6% growth as a target. China's aim is a stable population of 1.2 billion. So although anti-natalist policies all involve the reduction of fertility levels, the total reduction aimed for varies considerably amongst nations.

Differences among developing countries in the evolution of population policies are profound. In sub-Saharan Africa few countries have yet to take the first steps in formulating a population policy, whereas in East Asia political commitment to fertility control measures is high.

(a) Sub-Saharan Africa

Sub-Saharan Africa has the fastest population growth rate and highest fertility in the world, and yet few countries in this region have clear policies to reduce rapid population growth. Kenya was the first country to adopt such policies in 1967, followed by Ghana in 1969 and Mauritius in the early 1970s. However, the results have not been spectacular. Between 1965 and 1987 the fertility rate in Kenya decreased slightly from 8.0 to 7.7, and similarly over the same period the fertility rate in Ghana decreased from 6.9 to 6.4. Although about half the governments in sub-Saharan Africa provide family planning services for health and human rights reasons, few have an explicit demographic purpose. Twelve countries do not have anti-natalist population policies and do not support family planning services. These countries, including Chad, Gabon, Guinea Conakry, Côte d'Ivoire, Niger and Burkina Faso, are mostly in French-speaking Africa and have inherited colonial anti-contraception laws which are still in force.

(b) Latin America and the Caribbean

Population growth is rapid throughout Latin America and the Caribbean, although population policies have helped reduce fertility in a few countries. In 1966 Colombia supported family planning and in 1973 the Mexican government adopted an anti-natalist policy. Between 1965 and 1987 fertility fell from 6.3 to 3.2 in Colombia and from 6.7 to 3.6 in Mexico. By contrast, in Brazil, a country which had not committed itself to an anti-natalist policy, fertility over the same period dropped by less than 2.0%. Until 1974 the official Brazilian policy on population was pro-natalist, the argument being that Brazil would benefit from a large growing population to complement its vast territory and natural resources. However in 1974 the government approved a number of state level family planning programmes. In 1984 the government announced that a broad new health programme for women would include family planning assistance as part of a full range of maternal and child health care. The result has been a decline in fertility from 4.9 in 1978 to 3.5 in 1987.

(c) South Asia

One quarter of the world's population live in South Asia, and despite the fact that these countries have some of the lowest incomes in the world, fertility in the region

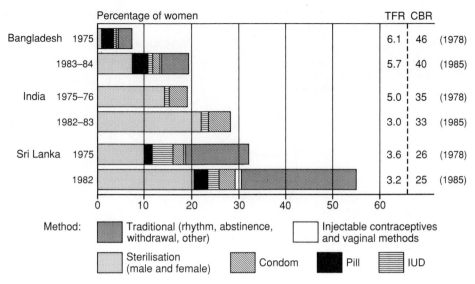

Figure 6.1　Percentage of married women aged 15–49 years using contraceptives, by method, in Bangladesh, India and Sri Lanka (Source: World Bank, 1980; 1984; 1987)

has fallen substantially. In Sri Lanka, for example, fertility has fallen from 4.9 in 1965 to 2.7 in 1987, while in India over the same period fertility has dropped from 6.2 to 4.3. Bangladesh and Pakistan have experienced more modest declines. Figure 6.1 shows contraceptive use in Bangladesh, India and Sri Lanka. In all three countries fertility has declined, the largest decline occurring in India. However, although declines have been accompanied by increased use of contraception, the figures show that contraceptive use is not the only factor to explain the declines. The reason for the success of anti-natalist policies in this region is the continued progress in female literacy. Increased female literacy is positively related to reductions in fertility. The mechanism for the reduction is complex, but the evidence shows that infant mortality rates decrease as female literacy increases. The fact that more children survive depresses the birth rate and encourages the use of contraception (see Chapter 4, section 2). However, despite progress in raising female literacy in this region, rates are still low. The Indian census of 1991 reports only 39% of women as literate, compared with 64% of men. It would therefore appear that fertility decline in this region is the result of a combination of factors, including an increase in female literacy and decrease in infant mortality rate. It is accompanied by increasing availability and acceptance of family planning programmes by couples.

(d) East Asia

The countries of East Asia have experienced marked declines in fertility in the last decade and now have the lowest fertility and natural growth rates of any developing region. The most dramatic reduction occurred in China where between 1965 and 1987 fertility rates fell from 6.4 to 2.4. Thailand has achieved a similar result over

181

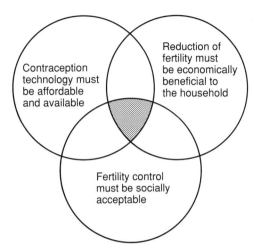

Figure 6.2   Conditions necessary for the successful implementation of an anti-natalist population policy

the same period, reducing its fertility from 6.3 to 2.8. Indonesia and the Philippines have also recorded significant declines. Anti-natalist population policy is more developed in this region than in any other and political commitment to reduce population growth is high. Family planning programmes are well established, and most countries have been successful in improving the socio-economic conditions necessary for fertility decline. Female literacy is high and infant mortality rates have been halved over the last twenty years. The experience of anti-natalist policies in the region is encouraging.

Where family planning services are widespread and affordable, for example in China, Columbia, India, Indonesia, Mexico, Sri Lanka and Thailand, fertility has declined more rapidly than social and economic progress alone would predict (see Demographic Transition Model in Chapter 2). However, in a number of countries, especially in Africa, the introduction of family planning programmes has not brought about the desired reduction in fertility. The success of an anti-natalist policy is dependent on the presence of certain conditions within society, as shown on Figure 6.2. Introducing affordable and accessible contraceptives is only part of the solution. In addition it must be economically beneficial to the family to have fewer children (see Wealth Flows Theory, Chapter 4) and small families must be socially acceptable. If either of these socio-economic conditions is not met then undue pressure may be exerted on couples to have more children.

3.   The role of family planning programmes

Family planning programmes not only make responsible parenthood easier by giving women control over their own fertility, they also bring substantial health benefits to mothers and children. Family planning is among the most basic of preventative

182

health care strategies, although it is rarely recognised as such. By enabling women to have fewer and more widely spaced births, it can help reduce maternal mortality from abortions and complications at childbirth, which currently kill 500 000 women annually worldwide. In addition, babies tend to be healthier and of a higher birth weight if they are spaced at least 24 months apart. Figure 6.3 shows the percentage

Figure 6.3   Percentage of infant deaths avoidable by birth spacing of a minimum of 24 months (Source: UNICEF, 1984; 1987)

% of deaths avoidable	Crude birth rate (1985)	Fertility rate (1985)
Syria 76	44	6.2
Panama 49	26	3.2
Peru 46	33	4.3
Kenya 41	54	7.8
Mexico 36	33	4.3
Pakistan 27	44	6.1
Indonesia 23	32	4.1
Sri Lanka 20	25	3.2
Nepal 18	43	6.3
Thailand 17	26	3.2
Lesotho 10	41	5.8

Plate 6.2   Birth control information in the Third World is increasingly being conveyed by television and film. Here in India, an educational film concerning birth, family planning and marriage is being promoted. (Photograph: G. O'Hare)

of infant deaths that could be avoided by birth spacing. Thus family planning programmes can contribute to reductions in the infant mortality rate. Family planning programmes can also help in detection, treatment and education concerning sexually transmitted diseases. These services therefore have a humanitarian role to play as well as comprising a necessary component of anti-natalist policy programmes.

(a) Geography of contraceptive use

Differences in contraceptive use among countries and regions is striking, as shown in Figure 6.4. In Europe and the USA contraceptive use among married women aged 15–45 is over 70%. In East Asia usage rates exceed 66%; however, in Asia as a whole usage rates of 30% are more common. In Latin America and the Caribbean rates of 40% are recorded, while the rate in North Africa and the Middle East is 20%. Sub-Saharan Africa has the lowest contraceptive usage rate of less than 10%. There is a strong correlation between contraceptive use and level of socio-economic development. For instance in the Third World the countries with the highest levels of contraceptive use are found in Latin America and Asia, where socio-economic levels are increasing (see Table 6.3). In Latin America contraceptive use is over 50% in Colombia, Costa Rica, Jamaica, Panama and Trinidad and Tobago. In Asia prevalence is over 50% in Korea, Sri Lanka and Thailand. The rate for Hong Kong and Singapore is over 70%. The lowest rates are found in Africa, with rates of less than 5% occurring in Cameroon, Côte d'Ivoire, Mauritania, Senegal and Somalia. The highest usage rates of contraceptives in Africa are found in Tunisia (31%), Egypt (24%), Benin (18%) and Zimbabwe (14%). However, within countries usage can be skewed towards certain groups of women. Studies consistently indicate that educated woman in their thirties, especially those living in urban areas who already have some children, are more likely to use contraceptives than poorly educated rural women.

(b) Contraceptive methods used

In most countries modern methods of contraception are popular. The World Fertility Survey which covered 41 countries in Asia, Africa, the Middle East, Latin America and the Caribbean found that in most of the countries surveyed, at least half the contraceptive users relied on oral contraceptives, IUDs or voluntary female sterilisation. The IUD is the most common form of contraception. More than 83 million women worldwide rely on this form of birth control (75% of whom live in China). Although modern methods often dominate, the method mix varies greatly between regions and countries.

Table 6.4 contrasts the type of contraception used by women in the developed and developing countries. In the developed countries, traditional methods, including abstinence, withdrawal and the rhythm method are the most common form of contraception. This is followed by the use of condoms and oral contraceptives. In the developing countries the most favoured form of contraception is sterilisation, followed by oral contraceptives and injectable ovulation depressants. However, within the developing countries there are differences. Figure 6.5 illustrates the

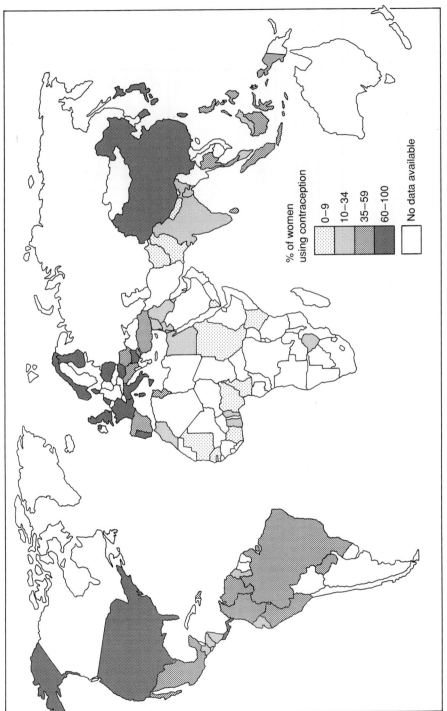

Figure 6.4   World distribution of women of reproductive age (15–49 years) who use any type of contraception (Source: World Bank, 1984)

% of women
using contraception

0–9
10–34
35–59
60–100

No data available

Table 6.3 Percentage of couples using contraceptives in developing countries, relating strength of family planning programme to socio-economic setting (Source: Illustration by Ian Worpole from 'The Growing Human Population' by Nathan Keyfitz. Copyright © 1989 by Scientific American, Inc. All rights reserved)

Socio-economic setting	1982 Family-planning programme strength								Mean
	Strong		Moderate		Weak		Very weak or none		
	country	percent	country	percent	country	percent	country	percent	
High	Hong Kong	80	Cuba	79	Costa Rica	66	Paraguay	36	
	Singapore	71	Panama	63	Brazil	50			
	Taiwan	70	Jamaica	55	Venezuela	49			
	Korea	58	Trinidad/Tobago	54	Peru	43			
	Colombia	51	Fiji	38	Chile	43			
	Mexico	40							
Mean		60		58		50		36	55
Upper middle	China	69	Thailand	58	Ecuador	40	Iran	23	
	Sri Lanka	57	Philippines	45	Turkey	40	Syria	20	
			Dominican Rep.	43	Honduras	27	Ghana	10	
			Malaysia	42	Egypt	24	Nicaragua	9	
			El Salvador	34	Morocco	19	Zaire	3	
			Tunisia	31	Guatemala	18	Zambia	1	
					Algeria	7			
Mean		63		42		25		11	30

Lower middle	Indonesia 48	India 32, Vietnam 21	Haiti 19, Zimbabwe 14, Kenya 7, Pakistan 6, Papua New Guinea 5, Senegal 4, Liberia 1	Bolivia 24, Nigeria 6, Lesotho 6, Burma 7, Cameroon 2, Uganda 1, Kampuchea 0	
Mean	48	27	8	6	12
Low		Bangladesh 19	Nepal 7, Tanzania 1	Benin 18, Sudan 5, Sierra Leone 4, Ethiopia 2, Somalia 2, Yemen 1, Burundi 1, Chad 1, Guinea 1, Malawi 1, Mali 1, Niger 1, Burkina Faso 1, Mauritania 1	
Mean		19	4	3	4
Mean	59	44	23	7	26

Table 6.4   Types of contraceptives used by married women aged 15–44 years (Source: New Internationalist, October 1987)

	Developed countries average %	Developing countries average %	China %
Sterilisation	14	47	35
Oral contraceptives and injectables*	23	23	9
Intra-uterine devices (IUD)	7	9	49
Condom	24	6	3
Traditional	32	15	4

* Injectables are not available in most developed countries, due to medical risks to the user.

methods of contraception used by married women, by age, in three contrasting countries, South Korea, NE Brazil and Zimbabwe. These diagrams demonstrate the importance of female sterilisation in Latin America, particularly amongst older women. This contrasts with Zimbabwe, where female sterilisation is much lower. In South Korea although female sterilisation is important, male sterilisation is also significant, perhaps representing a cultural difference between these countries. The oral contraceptive is most favoured by younger women and is most widely used in Zimbabwe and least used in South Korea. In all three countries withdrawal and rhythm methods are significant, however, other traditional methods are much more common in Zimbabwe than the other two countries. Only in South Korea do more than 5% of married women rely on condoms for protection.

In regions and countries where modern contraceptives are not available, induced abortion may be used as a method of reducing births. Until recently this was the case in Eastern Europe where contraceptives were often officially proscribed in accord with pro-natalist policies (see case study at the end of this chapter). In 1984, for example, 92 abortions were performed for each 100 live births in Bulgaria. This was one of the highest rates in the world. Abortion is also used in some West European countries to limit fertility, for example in Italy twice as many abortions were performed per 100 live births as in England and Wales (39 as opposed to 21) in 1984.

There are thus spatial differences in the type of contraceptive used. This often reflects government policy which dictates availability and cultural preferences. In South Asia for example, family planning services emphasise sterilisation and neglect reversible methods. This is especially the case in India and Sri Lanka (see Figure 6.1). In some countries where female literacy is low, oral contraception may have high failure rates due to misuse and is therefore not prescribed. In countries where female status is low, injectable contraceptives may be favoured by women who wish to conceal efforts to control their fertility from their husbands. For some couples cultural beliefs may dictate that withdrawal and rhythm techniques are used. For some women the only alternative to an unwanted pregnancy is induced abortion.

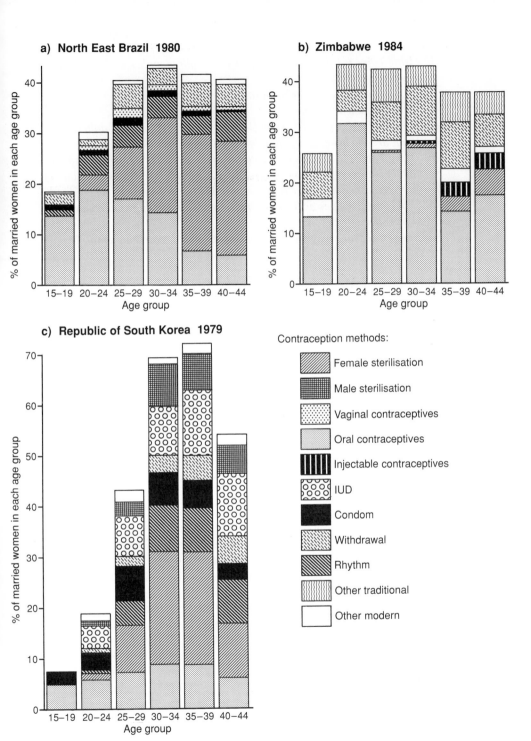

Figure 6.5   The methods of contraception used by married women, by age, in South Korea, North-East Brazil and Zimbabwe (Source: World Bank, 1984)

ASSIGNMENTS

1. (a) *Using Table 6.1 as a basis, suggest what indirect policies can be used by governments:*
     i) *to encourage higher birth rates;*
     ii) *to reduce birth rates.*
   (b) *How may direct policies be used by government population policies?*
2. (a) *What are the benefits of a family planning programme?*
   (b) *Using Table 6.3 discuss the relationship between the implementation of family planning programmes and the socio-economic status of a country.*
   (c) *With reference to Figure 6.5, compare the use of female sterilisation and oral contraceptives as forms of birth control in the three countries illustrated.*
   (d) *Suggest reasons why the type of contraceptive used varies spatially.*

B. Government Policies concerning Population Distribution

As with population growth, government policies can be very influential in changing population distribution patterns. Few countries have adopted explicit and coherent policies on population distribution, although many governments have economic goals which indirectly affect distribution. There are, however, a number of Third World countries which are increasingly using coercive policies to alter population patterns.

1. Indirect policies

Most governments, especially in the developed world, influence population distribution indirectly through regional development policies and planning regulations. Such legislation gives governments the power to control economic development. Many policies enable governments to restrain industrial and economic growth in specified metropolitan areas and encourage growth in peripheral regions. The relocation of employment opportunities in association with housing availability can be a strong magnet to population relocation. The UK is an excellent example of how such economic planning can indirectly alter population patterns.

Since 1945 successive legislation such as the Special Areas Act (1934) and the Distribution of Industry Act (1945) has enabled the British government to control regional economic development. In addition, through the New Towns Act (1946) and the Town and Country Planning Act (1947), the government also influences the spatial distribution and supply of new housing. By such methods the British government is able indirectly to alter population distribution. For example, since the Second World War, twenty-eight new towns have been built in England and Wales. These settlements have not only relieved population pressure on the large conurbations, but have also changed the settlement pattern of England and Wales (see Figure 6.6).

190

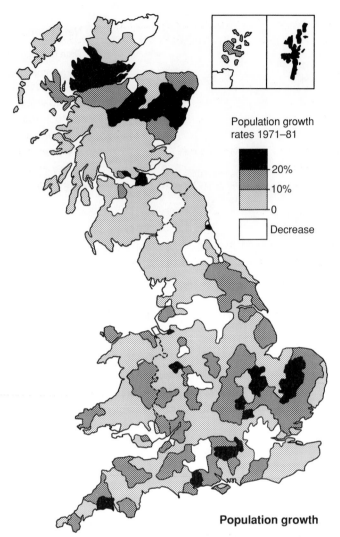

Population growth
rates 1971–81

■ 20%
▨ 10%
░ 0
□ Decrease

Population growth

Figure 6.6   New towns in Great Britain and population growth rates, 1971–1981 (Source: Hall, P. *Urban and Regional Planning*, 1982. Reprinted by permission of the Peters Fraser & Dunlop Group Ltd.)

Other European countries have similar policies which affect population distribution. In the Netherlands, for example, the decision to drain the Zuider Zee and build settlements such as Almere, Lelystad and Zeewolde on the new polders, has altered the population distribution pattern of the country, by encouraging people to move from crowded cities such as Amsterdam. Thus very often policies designed to promote regional economic growth indirectly affect population distribution.

Indirect policies affecting population distribution also occur in many developing countries, very often aimed at reducing population flows to the larger cities. For

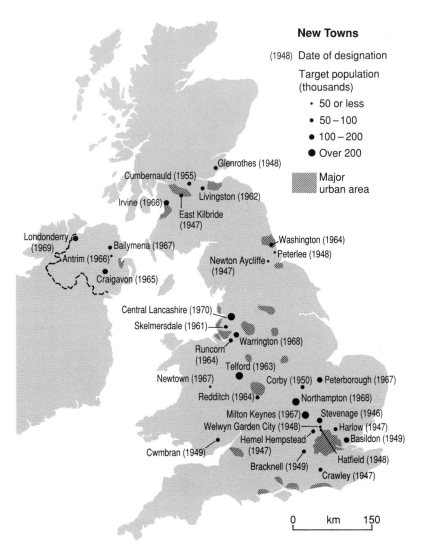

New Towns

(1948) Date of designation

Target population
(thousands)
• 50 or less
• 50 – 100
● 100 – 200
● Over 200

Major urban area

Glenrothes (1948)
Cumbernauld (1955)
Livingston (1962)
Irvine (1966)
East Kilbride (1947)
Londonderry (1969)
Ballymena (1967)
Antrim (1966)
Craigavon (1965)
Washington (1964)
Peterlee (1948)
Newton Aycliffe (1947)
Central Lancashire (1970)
Skelmersdale (1961)
Warrington (1968)
Runcorn (1964)
Telford (1963)
Newtown (1967)
Corby (1950)
Peterborough (1967)
Redditch (1964)
Northampton (1968)
Milton Keynes (1967)
Stevenage (1946)
Welwyn Garden City (1948)
Harlow (1947)
Basildon (1949)
Cwmbran (1949)
Hemel Hempstead (1947)
Hatfield (1948)
Bracknell (1949)
Crawley (1947)

0   km   150

Fig. 6.6 (cont'd)

example, many countries have invested in rural development projects including the provision of basic infrastructure such as clean water, roads, schools and clinics, in order to make the urban areas less attractive to potential migrants. Other countries have decided to relocate their capital cities. Both Brazil and Nigeria have begun constructing new capitals in central areas of low population density. The reasoning behind such decisions is not only to relieve the already over-crowded coastal cities, but also to try to encourage investment away from the existing growth poles. If the benefits of development are more evenly distributed, the flow of migrants to the coastal cities may be stemmed.

2. Coercive policies

Coercive policies concerning population distribution are more common in developing countries than in the West. These types of policies are very often associated with large scale development projects, particularly the building of dams which flood large areas of land. The Kainji Dam on the River Niger in Nigeria, for example, which was begun in 1964, not only flooded large areas of very fertile river valley but also displaced 44 000 people. These people were displaced physically, as well as suffering social and economic confusion and trauma. Similarly the Narmada Dam project in NW India will mean the uprooting of over one million people. Such projects necessitate the movement of large numbers of people, with little consultation and compensation. The result is an alteration of the population distribution pattern, with large numbers of people suffering displacement, in order to facilitate national economic development. Such policies are often condemned by pressure groups concerned with human rights.

ASSIGNMENTS
1. *Study Figure 6.6.*
   (a) Describe the pattern of New Town designations and proposed target populations in Great Britain.
   (b) Examine population growth rates in Great Britain 1971–81, and discuss the role New Towns may have played in the pattern.
   (c) What other factors may explain the population growth rates shown on Figure 6.6?

C. Case Studies

1. Anti-natalist population policies and the role of induced abortion in Eastern Europe

Although induced abortion cannot be classified as a form of contraception, it does reduce fertility by terminating unwanted pregnancies. In areas where modern contraceptives are not available, induced abortion may be the major form of birth control, and as such can have a significant impact on fertility levels. Abortion is not legal in all countries. For example in some countries in Africa, Latin America and the Middle East severely restrictive abortion legislation operates, allowing abortion only where the life of the woman is threatened. In some other parts of the world, for example, China and India, abortion legislation is more liberal, permitting abortion on demand. There have even been suggestions that in India, couples have chosen, after a sex test, to abort female foetuses. Between 1978 and 1983 it is estimated that 78 000 female foetuses were aborted because abortion is cheaper than paying a dowry. The practice is quite legal, even if morally questionable. Eastern Europe has some of the highest legal abortion rates in the world, only

Cuba, Japan, Singapore and USA have comparable rates. Figure 6.7 shows the legal abortion rates in Europe in the mid 1980s. From this map it is clear that the highest levels occur in Eastern Europe, followed by Northern and Western Europe.

Within Eastern Europe the incidence of legal abortion has varied widely over time and between countries, depending on government policies. Table 6.5 shows the chronology of legislation concerning induced abortion in four Eastern European countries. Bulgaria, Czechoslovakia and Romania all liberalised abortion in the late 1950s. East Germany was more cautious, liberalising its laws in the 1960s. The

Figure 6.7   Distribution of total legal abortion rates in Europe, 1985 (Source: UN Demographic Yearbook, 1988; Frejka, 1983)

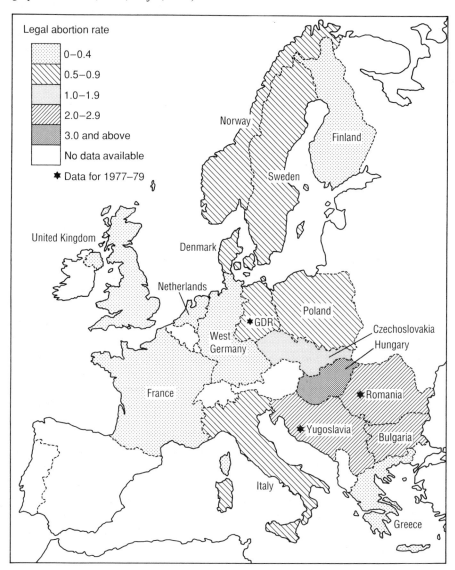

Table 6.5   Chronology of changes in abortion legislation in Eastern European countries, 1947–1974 (Source: Frejka, 1983)

Country	Month and year of implementation	Type of law/policy
Bulgaria	Apr. 1956	Abortion on request
	Jan. 1968	Moderate restriction (gradually relaxed)
	May 1972	Further restriction
	Apr. 1973	Further restriction on availability
	Feb. 1974	Moderate liberalisation (1972/73 restrictions reversed)
Czechoslovakia	Dec. 1957	Broad liberalisation
	Dec. 1962	Restrictive interpretation
	July 1966	Liberalised interpretation
	May 1973	Tightened administrative regulations
German Dem. Rep.	1947	Moderate liberalisation
	Sept. 1950	Restriction
	Mar. 1965	Liberalised interpretation
	Mar. 1972	Abortion on request
Romania	Sept. 1957	Abortion on request
	Oct. 1966	Broad restriction
	Apr. 1973	1966 decree slightly modified

fertility decline which occurred in Eastern Europe in the 1960s and early 1970s was presumed to be linked to the liberalisation of abortion, and as a result a number of governments reacted by imposing more restrictive abortion legislation at the same time as introducing other pro-natalist policies.

It is changes in government policy which explain the changing levels of abortion in Eastern Europe since 1950. These changes are shown on Figure 6.8. The pattern is clearly influenced by changes in legislation. In both Czechoslovakia and East Germany the total abortion rate increased abruptly after liberalisation in 1957 and 1972 respectively. The data for Romania shows that the total abortion rate increased rapidly following liberalisation in 1957, reaching a peak of 7.5 in 1965. This extremely high level caused grave public concern and in 1966 severely restrictive legislation was imposed. As a response the total abortion rate in Romania fell to only 1.5, but rose again in the 1970s to settle at between 2.0 and 2.15 per woman.

The enactment of restrictive abortion legislation in Eastern Europe brought about two consequences. First, there was an increase in the number of illegal abortions, as evidenced by a rise in deaths attributed to abortion. In 1966, following the introduction of restrictive legislation in Romania, deaths attributable to abortion increased seven-fold, and has continued to rise (see Figure 6.9). Secondly, fertility increased, as shown on Figure 6.10. The relationship between restrictive abortion legislation and increased fertility is confused by the fact that at the same time many

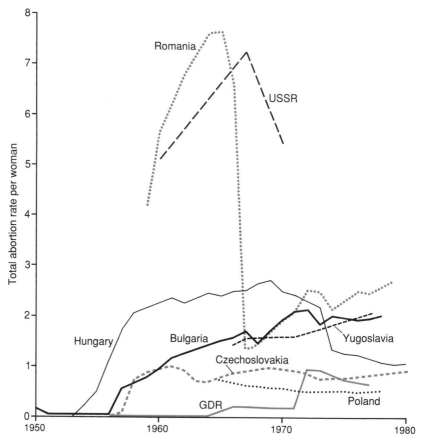

Figure 6.8   Total abortion rates in Eastern European countries, 1950–1980 (Source: Frejka, 1983)

governments introduced pro-natalist policies. But as Figure 6.10 shows there does appear to be a relationship between induced abortions and fertility in Eastern Europe.

The proportion of known pregnancies being terminated through legal abortion in Eastern Europe is shown in Figure 6.11. In the late 1970s over 50% of all pregnancies in Bulgaria, Romania and Yugoslavia were terminated by abortions, and in other East European countries the figure is approximately 30%. Poland had the lowest proportion of pregnancies terminated whilst Romania had the highest. These differences may be explained by the availability of modern contraceptives. Governments in this region have been very reluctant to introduce modern birth control techniques. In Bulgaria, Yugoslavia, Poland and Romania over 80% of the population use traditional birth control methods. In 1966 the situation was similar in Hungary, where no oral contraceptives or IUDs were available. However, by 1977 over 70% of married women used oral contraceptives or IUDs and only 25% rely on traditional methods. The availability of modern contraceptives in Hungary

Plate 6.3   Most of the children in Romanian orphanages are the product of unwanted pregnancies, which resulted from the government's pro-natalist policy. The children pictured in this orphanage are aged between 2 and 10 years and live in unheated, unsanitary conditions, with few toys and a limited education. What future do they have? (Photograph: Popperfoto/J.P. Key)

Figure 6.9   Known abortions and live births per 1,000 women aged 15 to 44 years, and deaths attributed to abortion per million women aged 15 to 44 years in Romania, 1955–1979 (Source: Frejka, 1983)

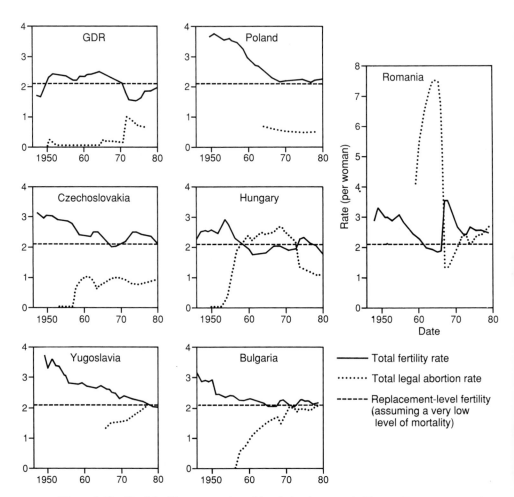

Figure 6.10   Total fertility rates and total legal abortion rates in Eastern European countries, 1946–1980 (Source: Frejka, 1983)

from the mid-1970s may explain the marked decrease in the number of abortions during this period (see Figure 6.10).

It is clear that the role of induced abortion in modifying fertility in Eastern Europe has been very significant, especially in the absence of modern family planning technology. However, the introduction and use of modern contraceptives may have a significant effect on reducing induced abortion rates in Eastern Europe.

2. Family planning policy reversal in Malaysia (anti to pro-natalist)

In 1957 the Federation of Malaya, comprising the eleven states of Peninsular Malaysia, gained its independence from British colonial rule. With the accession of

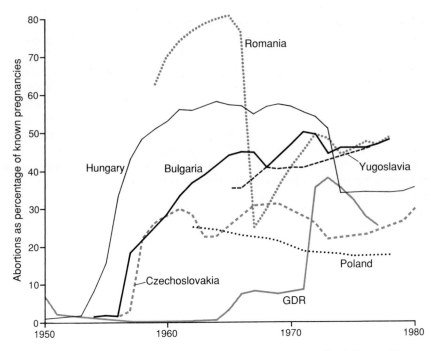

Figure 6.11   Legal abortions as a percentage of total known pregnancies in Eastern European countries, 1950–1980 (Source: Frejka, 1983)

Plate 6.4   The majority of Malays are rural based, many living in poor conditions. This is a Malay fishing village or *kampong* on the east coast of Malaysia. (Photograph: H.R. Barrett)

Sabah, Sarawak and Singapore in 1963, the federation became known as Malaysia. By mutual agreement with Singapore separated from Malaysia in 1965, becoming an independent sovereign state. The state of Malaysia covers an area of 329 479 square kilometres and in 1987 its population was 16.5 million. The population is not evenly distributed between the three regions, with over 83% of the Malaysian population living on the Peninsula, 9% on Sabah and the remaining 8% in Sarawak. It is a predominantly rural country (60% of the population live in rural areas), although industrialising rapidly. Malaysia relies on the export of electronic components, petroleum, timber and rubber as its main sources of income.

The population trend for Malaysia is shown in Figure 6.12. From this graph it can be seen that there has been a steady increase in the total population of Malaysia since 1947. Until 1960 annual average population growth rates were high, with rates of 2.5% and 2.8% recorded for the periods 1947–57 and 1957–60 respectively. This was in line with government policy, which considered high population growth rates to be an essential pre-condition for economic development. However, following an economic review in 1963 this pro-natalist policy was changed. The social, economic and health care problems associated with high population growth were cited as reasons for this reverse.

In response to this change in population policy, the Malaysian government established the National Family Planning Board (NFPB) in 1966. Although the NFPB pledged to improve the health and welfare of the family, its immediate aim was to reduce the annual population growth rate by 2% by 1985. In order to

Figure 6.12 Total population, crude birth rate and annual average growth rate in Malaysia, 1947–1987 (Source: World Bank, 1980; 1989)

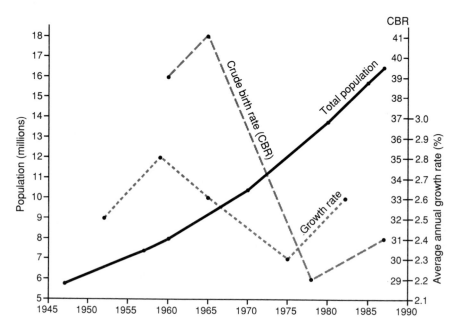

achieve this decrease in the growth rate, the NFPB aimed to reduce the birth rate to 6 per 1000. In addition, the programme pledged to improve the health and welfare of the family. In reality the NFPB concentrated mainly on reducing the birth rate, which it did by setting up family planning clinics and distributing contraceptives. Its main geographical focus of activity was the metropolitan and urban areas. After 1970 the programme was extended to rural areas, where family planning clinics were integrated with the maternal and child health services. By the mid-1970s the NFPB was stressing integrated population development. Informal approaches were adopted, and projects such as parasite control and income generation were integrated with family planning. Over ten years the programme had evolved from one which provided only birth control advice and technology into a wider concept of family planning. This concept included the provision of specialised services such as marriage and genetic counselling, infertility treatment and cancer screening, population and family health education programmes. It also supported and implemented projects which improved the status of women and the quality of life of the lower income groups through income-generating activities.

The success of the programme was measured by a drop in the birth rate from 41 in 1965 to 29 in 1977. Fertility declined from 6.6 in 1957 to 3.7 in 1980 (in Peninsular Malaysia). As Figure 6.12 shows, the annual population growth rate also fell. Success can also be measured by the number of couples using contraceptives. In 1966, although 44% of married women aged 15–44 had some knowledge of family planning, only 8% were using contraceptives. By 1974/5 these figures had increased to 92% and 36% respectively. There were still differences in contraceptive usage between rural and urban areas. A survey undertaken in the late 1970s indicated that 99% of married women in urban areas knew about family planning, and 59% used contraceptives. In rural areas although 92% of married women knew about birth control, only 39% were using any form of contraception. This difference may be the result of a number of the socio-economic factors discussed in Chapter 4, but may also be related to the spatial coverage of family planning services.

In addition to the NFPB programme the Malaysian government introduced a number of disincentives to couples wanting large families. These included separate tax assessments for married women, encouraging non-working spouses to join the labour force. It was hoped that increased female labour force participation rates would reduce fertility. The government also limited maternal benefits to the first three children.

Since 1982 Malaysia has seen a major change in population policy. In that year the Malaysian prime minister announced publicly that the country could support a population of 70 million. Since that pro-natalist statement birth control has ceased to be emphasised and maternity benefits have been extended up to the fifth child, with tax concessions introduced for the fourth and fifth children. Official sources suggest that the target population of 70 million should be attained by the year 2100. The response to this reversal in policy has been an increase in the birth rate and consequently the population growth rate (see Figure 6.12). The need for a larger internal market to support Malaysia's recent industrialisation has officially been advanced as the principal reason for the new policy. Experts speculate, however, that the government may wish to strengthen its ethnic power base, by altering the racial balance of the country.

Malaysia is a multi-ethnic nation, which is the result of immigration over hundreds of years. There are three main ethnic groups: the Malays who arrived in the peninsula from continental South East Asia in approximately 1500 BC, the Chinese and the Indians. Although both the Chinese and the Indians have a long history of contact with the region, large-scale immigration of these peoples did not take place until the eighteenth and nineteenth centuries under British colonial rule. During the colonial period Chinese and Indian economic interests lay in rubber and tin production as well as in commerce and trade in the urban centres. The Malays, on the other hand, were principally rural dwellers, engaged in the subsistence sectors of the economy, including agriculture and fishing. By 1941, due to immigration, the Chinese population outnumbered the Malay population, however, by 1980 the Malays comprised 55% of the total Malaysian population, the Chinese 34% and the Indians 10%. The Malays, known as *bumiputera*, are constitutionally regarded as the indigenous inhabitants of the country, and the other ethnic groups are officially labelled as non-indigenous.

Although the Malay population exercise a dominant political role within the country, they own only a small proportion of the nation's corporate wealth and have only marginal representation among the professions. In 1969 serious inter-communal rioting occurred in the capital, Kuala Lumpur. The cause of the disturbances appeared to be Malay resentment of the Chinese community's economic prominence and the political threat of pro-Chinese electoral results in the recent general election. The riot precipitated the resignation of the prime minister and as a result the government committed itself to address the specific problems of the

Plate 6.5 Most Chinese and Indian Malaysians are urban based, many making a living from trading. This picture shows part of the vibrant China Town in the capital of Malaysia, Kuala Lumpur. (Photograph: H.R. Barrett)

Malays. A New Economic Policy was introduced, the aim of which was to ensure a more equitable distribution of national wealth. The New Economic Policy was to run for twenty years and would set requirements for Malay equity participation in companies as well as setting levels for Malay employment. Positive discrimination in favour of Malays was to take place in awarding government contracts and licences. Malays were to be given almost exclusive preferential recruitment opportunities in the civil service, as well as educational priority. The thrust of the policy was too improve the lot of the Malay population by positive discrimination and to bring about a complete racial restructuring of the economy.

The result of twenty years of the New Economic Policy in Malaysia is a very sensitive internal ethnic balance. It is a precarious balance, due to the differential fertility rates amongst the groups. In 1983, for example, Malays had the highest fertility rate of 4.53, followed by Indians (3) and Chinese (2.72). As Figure 6.13 shows, the highest reduction in fertility between 1957 and 1980 has been recorded for the Indian population and the lowest for the Malays. The official explanation for this difference is the lower level of acceptance of family planning amongst Malay couples. This can be partially explained by the fact that the Malays tend to be poorer, less educated and rural based. However, whatever the reasons there is no doubt that this new pro-natalist policy will accentuate fertility differences between the ethnic groups. The result will be strengthening of the Malay group making them more numerically dominant. This could prove extremely divisive to the future ethnic harmony of Malaysia. Population planning policies can therefore not only be used to alter absolute population growth rates, but as this example shows, can also indirectly alter ethnic balances and hence power bases within populations.

Figure 6.13 Total fertility rates by ethnicity in peninsular Malaysia, 1958–1986 (Source: Cleeves, 1990)

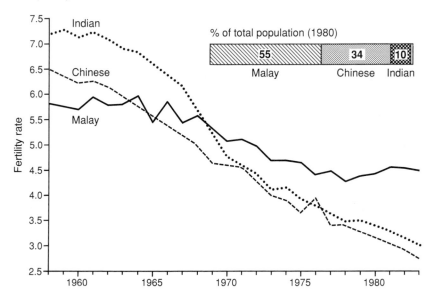

3.   Assisted resettlement in Newfoundland, Canada

The case of the redistribution of population in the Canadian Province of Newfoundland in the period 1954–1974 provides a rare example of a Western country actively encouraging and sponsoring resettlement in order to alter population patterns.

The island of Newfoundland, off the eastern seaboard of Canada, covers an area of 112 298 square kilometres. It is an inhospitable island with very rugged and rocky terrain and a harsh climate. In the late eighteenth century, immigrants of British and Irish ancestry settled on the island. As the main livelihood of these early settlers was fishing, most settled in sheltered coves around the island's 9600 kilometres of coastline, in order to exploit the excellent fishing grounds to the east and south of the island. These settlers lived in isolated communities, making a subsistence living from the inshore and cod fisheries, supplemented by sealing. In general when a village became overcrowded, families would move along the coast and establish a new settlement. As a result of the physical characteristics of the island and this pattern of isolated coastal settlement, most movement was by sea. Sea travel was itself limited by the small size of the fishing boats. In 1898 the trans-island railway was completed, but the absence of roads reconfirmed the necessity for coastal settlements. The 1921 census names 1300 settlements on the island and the 1945 census over 1200, of which more than half contained less than 100 people. So by 1949, when Newfoundland became confederated with its neighbour, Canada, the island had a settlement pattern of large numbers of small coastal fishing communities. This was consistent with the physical terrain of the island, its lack of roads, the subsistence nature of the economy and the low-technology fishing techniques employed by the population.

With confederation, the subsistence economy of the Newfoundlanders began to erode away. The influx of Federal money in the form of child allowances and pensions meant that many people used money for the first time. The Confederation brought with it roads (see Figure 6.14), electricity, telephones and modern schools and medical services. In addition, investment was attracted to the island in the form of timber and paper mills, mining and fish packing factories. This created year-round, on-shore employment in a number of key settlements.

The confederation with Canada and the spread of a cash economy coincided with a period of poor fishing seasons and people's rising aspirations. Thus when the authorities announced their intention to assist families from the more isolated villages to resettle nearer roads and other services, it received a positive response. The programme, administered by the Provincial Department of Public Welfare, gave grants of C$150 to each household in communities in which all families agreed to leave. Between 1954 and 1956, 185 communities comprising 8000 people took advantage of the resettlement programme. Many families moved only short distances, with resettlement being totally unplanned. Unfortunately many found that their economic situation did not improve after their move and there was some criticism of the scheme.

In 1965–67 the original scheme was replaced by the Fisheries Household Resettlement Programme, which was a joint Federal and Provincial scheme. Under

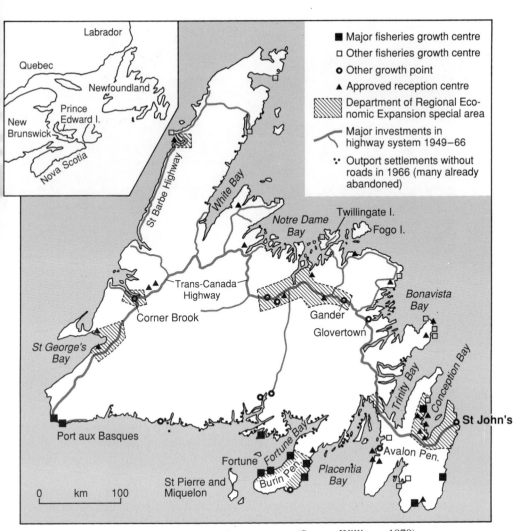

Figure 6.14   Newfoundland's road and settlement pattern (Source: Williams, 1979)

this programme grants of up to C$1000 were awarded per household, plus C$200 per dependant and removal costs. Families had to apply for this grant, which was only awarded when 90% of the community agreed to relocate. Under this programme, resettlement was to be steered, and suitable reception communities prepared. The aim was to shift the focus of resettlement from the previous social-welfare *push*, to an associated employment *pull*. To achieve this, growth centres were identified, usually those with fish packaging factories, and people were resettled in these communities (see Figure 6.14). The argument was that displaced fishermen would find it easier to find on-shore employment in these settlements. It also meant that services could be centralised. The stated aim of the scheme was to reduce the number of settlements on the island to 36, which would house about 500 000 people. An additional 200 villages would contain on average 1000 people each. In

Plate 6.6   An isolated village community on Newfoundland. This picture was taken in the late 1960s. This settlement is typical of those which have been resettled by the Canadian Government Assisted Resettlement Scheme. (Photograph: R.E. Pearson)

response to this programme, between 1965 and 1971 a further 18 000 people from 481 communities were resettled at a direct cost to the government of C$9 million. By the early 1970s enthusiasm for official sponsorship of resettlement was waning, and by 1974 resettlement had practically come to a halt.

Twenty years of officially sponsored resettlement in Newfoundland has had a tremendous impact not only on the distribution of population, but the size and distribution of settlements. Figure 6.15 shows the pattern of resettlement in southern Newfoundland for the period 1965–71. From this map it is clear that certain settlements have grown whilst others have disappeared. The towns of Burgeo and Fortune have gained population, whilst those settlements which are isolated from the road system have lost population. This redistribution of population can ultimately be traced back to the authorities' desire to provide modern facilities and services at a reasonable economic cost. At this level the scheme has been highly successful, but some academics claim that resettlement has meant a loss of access to the primary resource base of the island, its inshore fisheries, and has destroyed traditional culture and values. This case study provides an excellent example of the use of incentives by government to achieve a redistribution of population, in order to attain socio-economic goals.

ASSIGNMENTS

1. (a) *Using Table 6.5 and Figure 6.8 describe the link between government policy and levels of legal abortion in Bulgaria, Czechoslovakia, East Germany and Romania.*
   (b) *What impact did the introduction of restrictive abortion laws in these four countries have on, i) fertility and ii) deaths attributable to abortion?*
   (c) *Discuss the demographic impact of pro-natalist policies in Eastern Europe.*

206

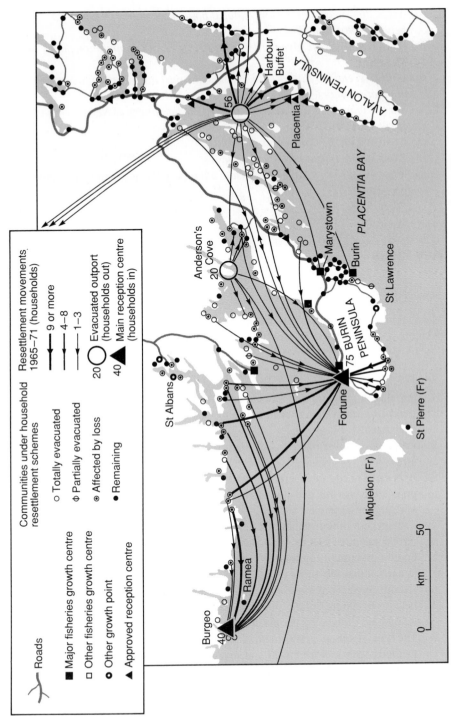

Figure 6.15 Resettlement in southern Newfoundland, 1965–1971 (Source: Williams, 1979)

207

2. (a) Assess the success of the anti-natalist population policy in Malaysia between 1966 and 1982.
   (b) What reasons were given in 1982 for the reversal of population policy in Malaysia?
   (c) With reference to Figure 6.13 examine the past and possible future effects of population policies on the ethnic balance of Malaysia.
3. (a) Study Figure 6.14 and describe the settlement pattern of Newfoundland in, i) 1966 and ii) 1979.
   (b) Comment on the differences identified.
   (c) Examine the reasons for these changes.
   (d) What are the advantages and disadvantages of this assisted resettlement programme?

Key Ideas

Introduction

Many governments, concerned by population trends, have introduced population planning policies that can influence the size, growth and distribution of populations.

A. Policies concerning population growth

1. Population growth policies can have direct and indirect effects on population trends, by introducing incentives and disincentives which can affect fertility decisions.
2. Pro-natalist government policies are those which seek to increase population size.
3. Anti-natalist policies are introduced by governments wishing to reduce population growth and are often associated with the introduction of family planning programmes.
4. The success of anti-natalist policies varies spatially, being least successful in Africa and most successful in Eastern Asia.
5. Family planning programmes provide the technology and advice for couples to control their fertility.
6. Family planning programmes are also important in preventative healthcare, helping to reduce infant and maternal mortality rates as well as identifying, treating and educating people concerning sexually transmitted diseases.
7. The type of contraceptive method used by couples varies spatially. Traditional methods such as withdrawal and rhythm are more common in the developed countries, while modern methods, such as female sterilisation and oral contraceptives, are favoured in the developing countries.
8. Within countries the level of female education and area of residence (i.e. rural or urban) appear to have a significant impact on contraceptive usage rates.

B. Government policies concerning population distribution

1. Government policies concerning population distribution can be very influential in altering population patterns.
2. Population patterns can be modified either directly, using coercive methods or indirectly, through regional economic policy.

C. Case Studies

1. In the absence of modern contraceptive technology, anti-natalist policies in Eastern Europe in the 1950s and 1960s were largely associated with the liberalisation of induced abortion legislation.
2. A change to pro-natalist policies in the late 1960s and early 1970s resulted in a tightening up of this legislation.
3. The result of this was an increase in the number of illegal abortions performed, an increase in female deaths associated with abortions and only a temporary increase in the crude birth rate.
4. Between 1960 and 1982 the Malaysian National Family Planning Board was successful in reducing fertility by almost 50%.
5. In 1982 the country adopted an ambitious pro-natalist policy aimed at increasing the population from 17 to 70 million.
6. The result of this policy has been to emphasise the difference in the fertility rates between the three main ethnic groups (Malay, Chinese and Indian), which in turn has brought about ethnic tension.
7. Since 1954 Newfoundland has attempted to resettle some of it isolated coastal population to designated growth areas.
8. The programme is regarded as a highly successful example of a non-coercive policy (in association with incentives), aimed to alter population distribution patterns.

Additional Activities

1. (a) Using Table 6.6 and Figure 6.16, analyse China's demographic patterns between 1949 and 1983.
   (b) Figure 6.17 shows the age/sex structure of the Chinese population in 1982. What are the implications of a continuing low birth rate for the future population of China?
   (c) Can the demographic experience of China be explained by the Demographic Transition Model discussed in Chapter 2?
2. (a) Re-read Chapters 2 and 4 and make a list of the components necessary for the implementation of a successful population planning programme.
   (b) Discuss each item on your list.
   (c) Go to your local Family Planning Clinic and assess its performance against your list.

(d) Find out all you can, from textbooks as well as newspaper and magazine reports, about the Population Planning Programme of a developing country. Assess its performance against your list (b).
3. 'Population planning policies, although inhibiting the freedoms of the individual, act in the best interests of society as a whole.' Discuss this statement using examples from the text.

Table 6.6   Main events affecting population trends in China since 1949 (Source: adapted from Jowett, 1986)

1949–1956	Sterilisation prohibited.
	Strict control on induced abortion.
	Mortality decline main thrust of population policy.
1956–1958	First family planning campaign with limited government support.
1958–1962	'Great Leap Forward'
1960–1961	Nationwide famine
1962–1966	Introduction of family planning projects in larger urban areas.
	Organised production and distribution of contraceptives.
1966–1969	'Cultural Revolution'
1970–present	Intensive family planning programme.
1970–1977	Urban families allowed 2 children
	Rural families allowed 3 children
1977	All families restricted to 2 children
1979	One couple, one child policy introduced.

Figure 6.16   Crude birth rates, crude death rates and population totals for China, 1949–1983 (Source: Jowett, 1986)

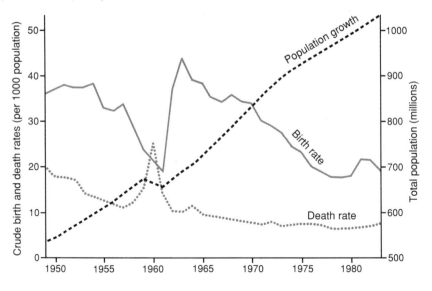

210

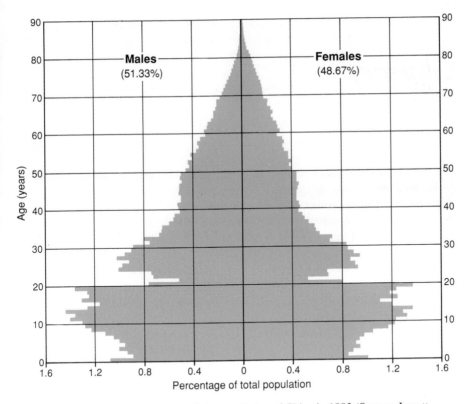

Figure 6.17   Age and sex structure of the population of China in 1982 (Source: Jowett, 1986)

Glossary

Age-specific mortality rate Number of deaths of persons of a certain age per 1000 of the population in that age group.

Age structure The age composition of a population.

Anti-natalist policy A policy seeking to decrease population growth.

Carrying capacity The number of people that can be sustained by a natural system, without destroying that system.

Chemotherapy Treatment by chemically mass-produced drugs.

Contraception Any practice deliberately undertaken to reduce the risk of conception.

Crude Birth Rate (CBR) Number of births in a specific period per 1000 of the population.

Crude Death Rate (CDR) Number of deaths in a specific period per 1000 of the population.

Dependency ratio The ratio of unproductive members of the population i.e. the young (less than 15) and elderly (over 60/65) to the population of working age (15–60/65).

Epidemiology Study of the causes, consequences and distribution of disease and death in human populations.

Fertility rate The number of children that would be born to 1000 women passing through the child bearing years, assuming none of the women die.

Induced abortion Any practice that deliberately interrupts the normal course of gestation.

Infant Mortality Rate (IMR) The number of deaths of infants under one year old per 1000 live births in a given year.

Life expectancy The average number of years that would be lived by a group of people born in the same year, assuming that age-specific death rates of that year are maintained throughout the life history of the group.

Migration The permanent or semi-permanent change in residence of an individual.

Mobility Short-term repetitive and cyclical movements as well as migration.

Overpopulation When the population of an area exceeds the carrying capacity of the area, resulting in environmental degradation.

Polygamy Where a man has more than one wife at the same time.

Population momentum Population growth which is the result of large numbers of people in reproductive age group, despite falling fertility rates.

Population planning policies Measures explicitly and implicitly instituted by a government, that influence population size, growth and distribution.

Population pyramid Visual expression of the age and sex structure of a population at a given time.

Post-partum abstinence Prolonged abstinence from sexual relations while a newborn baby is breast-feeding.

Pro-natalist policy Policy seeking to increase population growth.

Proximate determinants The biological factors influencing fertility, which may be affected by socio-economic factors. They include marriage patterns, patterns of sexual activity, duration of breast-feeding, induced abortions, levels of sterility, contraceptive use.

Sanitary reforms Aim to eliminate those environmental conditions favourable to the spread of disease and include the provision of safe sewage disposal and clean water supplies.

Sex ratio index Number of males per 100 females.

Standardised Death Rate (SDR) Indicates what the CDR would be if the population being studied had the same age and sex structure as a population that is being used as the standard.

Sterility The inability to conceive or carry a child.

Sustainable population The optimal number of people that a biological system can support without degradation.

Total fertility rate per woman Fertility rate divided by 1000 to give the number of children per woman in child bearing years.

References and Further Reading

Findlay, A. & Findlay, A. (1987) *Population and Development in the Third World*, Methuen, London.
Hall, R. (1989) *World Population Trends*, Cambridge University Press, Cambridge.
Jones, H. (1990) *Population Geography*, Paul Chapman Publishing, London.
Unicef Annual *The State of the World's Children Yearbook*, Oxford University Press, Oxford
United Nations (1989) *World Population at the Turn of the Century*, United Nations, New York.
Matthews, H & Foster, I. (1989) *Geographical Data Sources, Presentation and Analysis*, Oxford University Press.

Chapter 1

Ackerman, E.A. (1970) 'Population, Natural Resources and Technology'. In Demko G.J. et.al. (eds.) *Population Geography: a reader*, McGraw-Hill Books, New York.
Clarke, J. (1972) *Population Geography*, Pergamon, Oxford.
Cross, N. (1990) *The Sahel: the Peoples' Right to Development*, Minority Rights Group, London
Boserup, E. (1965) *The Conditions of Agricultural Growth: the Economics of Agrarian Change Under Population Pressure*, Allen & Unwin.
Gorse, J.E. & Steeds, D.R. (1987) *Desertification in the Sahelian and Sudanian Zones of West Africa*, World Bank, World Bank Technical Paper 6, Washington.
Johnson, B.L.C. (1982) *Bangladesh*, Heinemann Educational, London.
Jones, H. (1990) *Population Geography*, Paul Chapman Publishing, London.
Lee, R.D. (1986) 'Malthus and Boserup: A Dynamic Synthesis'. In Coleman D. & Schofield R. (eds.) *The State of Population Theory*, Basil Blackwell, Oxford.
Malthus, T.R. (1970) 'A Summary View of the Principle of Population'. In Demko, G.J. et.al. (eds.) *Population Geography: a reader*, McGraw-Hill Books, New York.
Meadows, D.H. et.al. (1972) *The Limits to Growth*, Pan Books, London.
Myers, N. (1987) 'Population, Environment and Conflict', *Environmental Conservation*, 14, 15–22.
Shaw, R.P. (1989) 'Rapid Population Growth and Environmental Degradation: Ultimate Versus Proximate Factors', *Environmental Conservation*, 16, 199–208.
Woods, R. (1986) 'Malthus, Marx and Population Crises'. In Johnston, R.J. & Taylor, P.J. (eds.) *A World in Crisis? Geographical Perspectives*, Basil Blackwell, Oxford.
Woolmington, E. (1985) 'Small Maybe Inevitable', *Australian Geographical Studies*, 23, 195–207.

Chapter 2

Brown, L.R. & Jacobson, J.L. (1989) *Our Demographically Divided World,* Worldwatch Institute Paper 74
Chung, R. (1970) 'Space-time Diffusion of the Transition Model: the Twentieth Century Patterns'. In

Demko, G.J. et.al. (eds.) *Population Geography: a reader*, McGraw-Hill Books, New York.

Clarke, J.I. (1985) 'Islamic Populations: Limited demographic Transition', *Geography*, 70, 118–128.

Geographical Magazine, April 1989 (Evans).

Heenan, L.D.B. (1980) Teaching the Theory of Demographic Transition, *New Zealand Journal of Geography*, 68, 4–11.

Joshi, H. (ed.) (1989) *The Changing Population of Britain*, Basil Blackwell, Oxford.

Merrick, T.W. (1986) World Population in Transition, *Population Bulletin*, 41, 1–51.

Omran, A.R. (1971) 'The Epidemiologic Transition: a Theory of the Epidemiology of Population Change', *Milbank Memorial Fund Quarterly*, 49, 509–538.

Weeks, J.R. (1988) 'The Demography of Islamic Nations', *Population Bulletin*, 43, 1–55.

Zelinsky, W. (1971) 'The Hypothesis of the Mobility Transition', *Geographical Review*, 61, 219–249.

Chapter 3

Compton, P.A. (1985) Rising Mortality in Hungary, *Population Studies*, 39, 71–86.

Dyson, T. & Moore, M. (1983) On Kinship Structure, Female Autonomy, and Demographic Behaviour in India, *Population and Development Review*, 9, 35–60.

Hammond, E.I. (1977) Sex Differentials in Mortality, an Enquiry with Reference to the Arab Countries and Others, *World Health Statistics Report*, 30, 174–206.

Jones, H. (1990) *Population Geography*, Paul Chapman Publishing, London.

Mandle, J.R. (1970) The Decline in Mortality in British Guiana, 1911–1960, *Demography*, 7, 301–315.

McKeown, T. (1976) *The Modern Use of Population*, Edward Arnold, London.

Newland, K. (1981) *Infant Mortality and the Health of Societies*, Worldwatch Institute Paper, 47.

Teitelbaum, M.S. (1984) *The British Fertility Decline*, Princeton University Press, Princeton.

United Nations (1982) Infant Mortality: World Estimates and Projections, *Population Bulletin of United Nations*, 14, 31–53.

Woods, R. & Woodward, J. (eds.) (1984) *Urban Disease and Mortality in Nineteenth Century England*, Batsford Academic and Educational, London.

Chapter 4

Anker, P., Buvinic, M. & Youssef, N.H. (eds.) (1982) *Women's Roles and Population Trends in the Third World*, Croom Helm, London.

Bongaarts, J., Frank, O. & Lesthaeghe, R. (1984) The Proximate Determinants of Fertility in Sub-Saharan Africa, *Population and Development Review*, 10, 511–537.

Caldwell, J.C. (1982) *Theory of Fertility Decline*, Academic Press, London.

Davis, K. (1984) Wives and Work: the Sex Revolution and its Consequences, *Population and Development Review*, 10, 397–417.

Doenges, C.E. & Newman, J. L. (1989) Impaired Fertility in Tropical Africa, *Geographical Review*, 79, 99–111.

Frank, O. (1983) Infertility in Sub-Saharan Africa: Estimates and Implications, *Population and Development Review*, 9, 137–144.

Jones, H. (1990) *Population Geography*, Paul Chapman Publishing, London.

Joshi, H. (ed.) (1989) *The Changing Population of Britain*, Basil Blackwell, Oxford.

Population Information Program (1985) Fertility and Family Planning Surveys: an Update, *Population Report*, 13, M289–M348.

Teitelbaum, M.S. (1984) *The British Fertility Decline*, Princeton University Press, Princeton.

Van De Walle, E. & Knodel, J. (1980) Europe's Fertility Transition: New Evidence and Lessons for Today's Developing World, *Population Bulletin*, 34.

World Bank (1984) *World Development Report*, Oxford University Press, Oxford.

World Resources Institute (1987) *World Resources*, Basic Books, New York.

Chapter 5

Butterworth & Chance (1981) *Latin American Urbanization*, Cambridge University Press, Cambridge.

Champion, A.G. (1987) Recent Changes in the Pace of Population Deconcentration in Britain, *Geoforum*, 18, 379–401.

Geographical Magazine, December 1987 (Leatherby).

Jacobson, J.L. (1988) *Environmental Refugees: a Yardstick of Habitability*, Worldwatch Institute Paper 86.

Lawless, R. J. & Seccombe, I.J. (1986) The Middle East: A New Destination for Turkish Labour Immigration, *Tijdschrift voor Economic en Social Geografie*, 77, 251–257.

Lewis, G.J. (1982) *Human Migration*, Croom Helm, London.

Lewis, J.R. (1986) International Labour Migration and Uneven Regional Development in Labour Exporting Countries, *Tijdschrift voor Economic en Social Geografie*, 77, 27–41.

Morris, A.S. (1987) *South America*, Hodder and Stoughton, Sevenoaks.

Ogden, P.E. (1984) *Migration and Geographical Change*, Cambridge University Press, Cambridge.

Owen, R. (1985) *Migrant Workers in the Gulf*, Minority Rights Group Report 68, London.

Papademetriou, D.G. (1984) International Migration in a Changing World, *International Social Science Journal*, 36, 409–423.

Power, J. (1984) *Western Europe's Migrant Workers*, Minority Rights Group Report 28, London.

Van Amersfoort, H, Muss, P. & Penninx, R. (1984) International Migration, the Economic Crisis and the State: an Analysis of Mediterranean Migration to Western Europe, *Ethnic and Racial Studies*, 7, 238–267.

Vaughan-Williams P. (1981) *Brasil,* University Tutorial Press (now Unwin Hyman of HarperCollins Publishers Limited).

Weiner, M. (1990) Immigration: Perspectives from Receiving Countries, *Third World Quarterly*, 12, 140–165.

Chapter 6

Cleeves, P. (1990) Births, Marriages and Deaths in Penisular Malaysia, *Geographical Magazine*, February.

Frejka, T. (1983) Induced Abortion and Fertility: a Quarter Century of Experience in Eastern Europe, *Population and Development Review*, 9, 494–520.

Hall, P. (1982) *Urban and Regional Planning,* Penguin Books.

Jacobson, J.L. (1987) *Planning the Global Family*, Worldwatch Institute Paper, 80.

Jowett, A.J. (1986) China: Population Change and Population Control, *Geo Journal*, 12, 349–363.

Population Information Program (1985) Fertility and Family Planning Surveys: An Update, *Population Report*, 13, M289–M348.

World Bank (1984) *World Development Report*, Oxford University Press, Oxford.

Williams A.F. (1979) Newfoundlanders Move to Town, *Geographical Magazine,* December, 156–161.

Index